# Fortifying the Cloud: Strategies for Understanding and Mitigating Fault Tolerance Bugs

Jacksin

# Table of Contents

# Chapter 1: Introduction

The dependability of cloud systems is an important topic in both the computer science research and the technology industry. Among all the threats to cloud system dependability, software bugs in the fault tolerance routines are one of the most notorious. This book uses *fault tolerance bugs*, or *FTBugs*, to denote the bugs in the fault tolerance routines. FTBugs sabotage a cloud system's effort to tolerate faults at runtime, severely affecting the system dependability. Moreover, it is arduous to uncover all FTBugs during in-house testing because of various challenges in exposing and detecting FTBugs.

To protect the dependability of cloud systems, this book proposes to address FTBugs from three aspects, including understanding, detecting, and exposing FTBugs in cloud systems.

## 1.1 FTBugs in Cloud Systems

### 1.1.1 Cloud System Dependability is Important

Cloud systems are becoming increasingly important in our daily life. For example, a majority of Fortune 500 companies have adopted cloud storage to host their data [8, 11]. As another example, many of the online services we use everyday are also powered by the cloud [5, 35, 82]. Moreover, multiple studies have shown that the global cloud business has a revenue of hundreds of billions of U.S. dollars and the revenue growth is still accelerating [27,64].

As a result, the dependability of cloud systems becomes critical. Sometimes, cloud system failures cause severe financial loses. For instance, in 2017, a three-hour outage of Amazon Web Services caused 150 million U.S. dollar loss for S&P 500 companies [29]. At other times, the impact of a cloud system failure even goes beyond economy: In 2014, when Facebook service failed, several Los Angeles residents called 911 [10]. Indeed, a cloud system failure can have so much damage that news reports are tracking the worst cloud outages every year [93–96].

## 1.1.2 FTBugs Affect Cloud System Dependability

A commonly accepted model of the threats to system dependability is the *fault-error-failure* model proposed by Jean-Claude Laprie [70]: A *failure* occurs when the service delivered by a system deviates from the correct service. An *error* is the partial system state which leads to the subsequent failure. A *fault* is the cause of the error.

In cloud systems, various faults can occur. Natrual disasters can cause power outages of the host machines, switch failures can lead to network partitions that separate a cluster into disconnected sub-groups, and users can issue invalid requests to the cloud system, for example.

When a fault occurs, the cloud system will try to tolerate the fault to avoid failure. Figure 1.1 shows the general fault tolerance process. After a fault causes an error in the cloud system, the error propagation starts. The fault tolerance routines of a cloud system usually consist of error detection and error handling code in multiple system components. If the cloud system resumes correct execution after a component detects and handles the

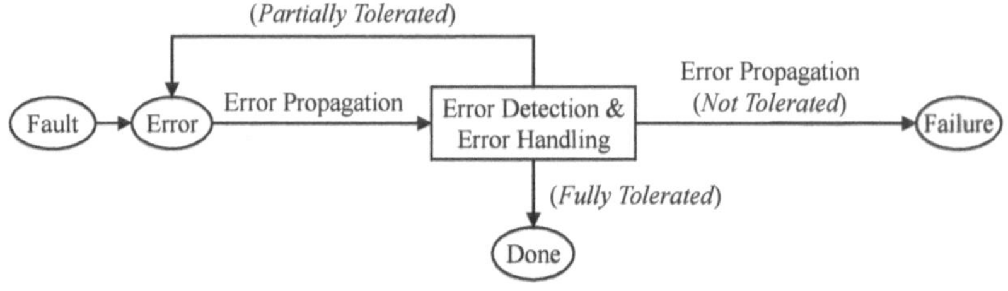



Figure 1.1: The General Process of Fault Tolerance in Cloud Systems.

error, the fault is *fully tolerated* and the fault tolerance process finishes. If the fault is only *partially tolerated* and other components still need to perform error handling, the cloud system will continue to propagate the error to those components. In the case where the fault is *not tolerated* by the cloud system, the error will be propagated out of the cloud system boundary, becoming a failure.

Although developers strive to design and implement fault tolerant cloud systems, faults can still cause cloud system failures due to bugs in the fault tolerance routines, i.e., the code for error propagation, error detection, and error handling. This book refers to bugs in the fault tolerance routine as *fault tolerance bugs*, or *FTBugs*.

Despite developers' efforts in testing their cloud systems [43, 49–51], some **FTBugs** still slip through the tests. A major reason is because the triggering process of these bugs often have strict requirements on the type, the location, and the timing of the triggering fault [2, 53]. As a result, FTBugs still exist in cloud systems and cause system failures in production runs [2, 37, 53, 59, 60, 74, 80]. Effective approaches to address FTBugs in cloud systems are direly needed.

## 1.2  Addressing FTBugs in Cloud Systems

### 1.2.1  Approaches to Address Software Bugs

Many different approaches have been proposed to address bugs in software systems. Most
of them fall within one of the following spectrums.

**Bug Prevention.**  Good programming language features can help developers prevent intro-
ducing bugs in the first place. For example, features like garbage collection free developers
from implementing low level functionalities that are prone to error. As another example,
features like the check-or-specify requirement in Java [85] guide developers to write programs in a more dependable way. However, since the types of bugs that can be prevented
using language features are still limited, other approaches are needed to further reduce bugs
in software systems.

**Bug Exposure and Bug Detection.**  Bug exposure and bug detection techniques aim at
uncovering bugs after they are introduced into the software. Bug exposure techniques try to
identify conditions under which bugs would be triggered. Bug detection techniques analyze
the source code or the execution of a software system to determine what and where the bug
is. While these two types of techniques have different focuses, they can benefit from each
other. Specifically, bug exposure techniques rely on bug detetcion techniques to determine
the manifestation of a bug. Moreover, many bug detection techniques require the bug to
be exposed before they can perform the analysis. Finally, static bug detetcion techniques
that only analyze the program source code may report false positives due to the absence of
concrete runtime information. Bug exposure techniques can help validate the reported bugs.
Both bug exposure and bug detection techniques are critical and widely used in practice.

**Bug Fixing.** After a bug is uncovered, either during in-house testing or in a production run, the bug needs to be fixed. Bug fixing is challenging since it requires identifying the root cause, proposing a solution (i.e., a patch), and verifying the correctness of the solution. It is worth noting that, the solution verification is often performed with the help of bug exposure and bug detection techniques.

**Understanding Bugs.** Finally, to effectively prevent, expose, detet, and fix bugs, a good understanding of the bugs being addressed is helpful. A characteristic study of software bugs is a common approach to obtain such an understanding.

Among the above mentioned approaches for addressing software bugs, this book focuses on understanding, detecting, and exposing FTBugs in cloud systems. §1.2.2 summarizes the state-of-the-art in understanding, detecting, and exposing FTBugs. §2 zooms in each type of techniques and provides more details.

### 1.2.2 State of The Art in Understanding, Detecting and Exposing FT-Bugs in Cloud Systems

A good understanding of software bugs is critical for effectively addressing bugs in software systems. In the past, many characteristic studies [59, 60, 74, 101] on bugs in cloud systems have shown that FTBugs are one of the most common root causes of cloud system failures. Several studies [2, 53] focus on FTBugs triggerred by certain types of faults. However, few studies analyze the relation between the triggering fault and the triggered FTBug. This relation is helpful for designing effective approaches to address FTBugs in cloud systems.

Many techniques have been proposed to detect FTBugs. A majority of the proposed techniques [28, 31, 61, 65, 67, 68, 88, 89, 91, 101] focus on FTBugs in error detetcion and error handling routines. On the contrary, only a few tools [65, 67] detect incorrect error propagation. However, these tools only consider the case in which the error is not propagated. During error propagation, the propagated error must accurately represent the triggering fault so that appropriate error handling operations will be executed. Effective approaches to detect inaccurate errors are desired.

How to effectively expose FTBugs in cloud systems is an open problem. Many distributed model checkers [62, 71, 78, 100] detect FTBugs by exhausting the possible states of a cloud system. These approaches are intrinsically expensive due to their exhaustive nature. Several other approaches [1–4, 52, 75, 77, 86] adopt fault injection testing, which injects faults when testing a cloud system. Since cloud systems run on networked machines, network partition faults are inevitable and should be tolerated by cloud systems. However, only two of these proposed tools [2, 86] inject network partitions. Moreover, both tools require developers to specify when the network partition starts and stops. As a result, both tools are ineffective in exposing FTBugs whose triggering condition has strict timing requirements on the network partition. A more systematic approach for injecting network partitions can improve the effectiveness in exposing these bugs.

## 1.3 Book Contribution

This book addresses FTBugs in cloud systems from three directions: understanding FTBugs in cloud systems, detecting FTBugs that are caused by propagating an inaccurate error, and proposing a fault injection approach that systematically explores the starting point and the stopping point of a network partition to expose FTBugs in cloud systems.

### 1.3.1 Understanding FTBugs in Cloud Systems

Since exception mechanism is commonly used for fault tolerance in cloud systems, this book studies *eBugs*, i.e., bugs in using exception mechanism, to understand fault tolerance bugs in cloud systems. Specifically, the study analyzes 210 eBugs selected from six popular cloud systems, including Cassandra, HBase, HDFS, Hadoop MapReduce, YARN, and ZooKeeper. By examining the bug report and the fixing patch of each eBug, this study answers three important research questions: (i) How are eBugs triggered in cloud systems? (ii) What are the root causes of eBugs? (iii) What are the impacts of eBugs on cloud systems?

This study reveals that eBugs are severe in cloud systems: 74% of the studied eBugs affect system availability or integrity. More importantly, exposing eBugs through testing is possible: 54% of the studied eBugs are triggered by non-semantic conditions, such as network faults. Furthermore, 40% of the studied eBugs can be triggered by simulating the triggering faults at simple system states. Finally, findings from this study suggest that the type of the triggering faults are useful for detecting eBugs in cloud systems.

### 1.3.2 Detecting FTBugs in Cloud Systems

Although propagating an accurate error is the prerequisite of correct error detection and error handling, few existing techniques detect FTBugs caused by inaccurate errors. Moreover, our eBug study shows that a non-negligible proportion of the studied eBugs are *inaccurate exceptions*, which are caused by propagating an exception object that inaccurately represents the triggering fault. To address this problem, this book proposes DIET and DECAF, two techniques for detecting inaccurate exceptions in cloud systems. In cloud systems, an exception object usually has multiple *exception features* such as the exception class, the error message, and the program context. When these features have inconsistent values, the exception object is inaccurate. As a result, both DIET and DECAF detect inaccurate exceptions by identifying exception objects that have inconsistent feature values.

DIET employs a *supervised* approach to detect inaccurate exceptions. We find that the exception class and the error message of an inaccurate exception often imply different types of triggering faults. Based on this observation, DIET detects inaccurate exceptions by comparing the fault types implied by the class and the error message of an exception object. Specifically, DIET first learns from a set of labelled exception objects to understand which type of triggering fault an exception class or an error message implies. Then, DIET reports an inaccurate exception if the class and the error message of the exception object imply different types of faults. Using the exception instances curated from our eBug study as the training data, DIET detects 31 inaccurate exceptions in four popular cloud systems, namely, Cassandra, HBase, Hadoop, and ZooKeeper. 23 of the detected inaccurate exceptions have been confirmed by the developers of the evaluated systems.

DECAF employs an *unsupervised* approach to detect inaccurate exceptions. To determine the consistency of two exception feature values, DECAF checks how frequently these two values co-appear on an exception object. Values that rarely co-appear are likely inconsistent. Specifically, DECAF reports an inaccurate exception if the exception class, the error message, and the program context of an exception object rarely co-appear. Experiments on the same four target systems show that DECAF is also effective in detecting inaccurate exceptions: DECAF detects 77 inaccurate exceptions in the target systems. Comparing the inaccurate exceptions detected by DIET and DECAF shows that these two techniques are mostly complimentary.

### 1.3.3  Exposing FTBugs in Cloud Systems

Not all FTBugs can be detected statically due to the absence of runtime information. Another way to uncover FTBugs is to expose them through executing the program. However, it is challenging to expose some FTBugs because their triggering processes have strict timing requirements on the triggering faults. *Partition bugs*, i.e., FTBugs that are triggered by network partitions, can be especially hard to expose since their triggering processes can have strict requirements on both when a network partition starts and when a network partition stops. Moreover, as discussed in §1.2.2, existing techniques do not detect partition bugs effectively.

To address this problem, this book proposes CoFI, the first fault injection technique that controls both the starting point and the stopping point of the network partitions to test cloud systems. Specifically, CoFI controls the timing of the network partition to thoroughly exercise a cloud system in inconsistent states, where partition bugs are more likely to occur. Experiments with three widely-deployed cloud systems, i.e., Cassandra, HDFS, and YARN show that CoFI is effective in detecting bugs triggered by network partitions. Specifically, CoFI detects 12 previously-unknown bugs, and four of the detected bugs have been confirmed by developers.

## 1.4  Outline

The remainder of this book is organized as follows. Chapter 2 reviews prior work on addressing FTBugs in cloud systems. Chapter 3 presents the study on eBugs in cloud systems. Chapter 4 proposes DIET and DECAF, the two techniques for detecting inaccurate exceptions. Chapters 5 introduces CoFI, a novel approach for injecting network partitions to test cloud systems. Finally, Chapter 6 summarizes the book and discusses directions for future work.

The materials in some chapters have been published as conference papers. The materials in Chapter 3 and some materials in Chapter 4 have been presented in [21]. The materials in Chapter 5 have been presented in [22].

# Chapter 2: Background and Related Work

This chapter reviews previous work on addressing fault tolerance bugs, i.e., FTBugs, in cloud systems. §2.1 discusses previous characteristic studies on FTBugs in cloud systems. §2.2 summarizes existing techniques for detecting FTBugs. §2.3 lists prior work on exposing FTBugs in cloud systems. Finally, §2.4 briefly talks about other related works.

## 2.1 Understanding FTBugs in Cloud Systems

In the past, several bug studies are performed to understand what bugs exist in cloud systems. Yuan et al. study 198 cloud system failures and find that most catastrophic failures in cloud systems are caused by bugs in error detection and error handling routines [101]. Gunawi et al. analyze 3,655 issues in cloud systems and reveal that FTBug is the second most common cause for cloud system failures [59]. Liu et al. examine 112 high-severity production incidents in Microsoft Azure and observe that FTBug is the most common cause for the studied incidents [74]. All these studies suggest that FTBugs widely exist and are affecting the dependability of cloud systems.

Some other studies focus on FTBugs that are triggered by specific types of faults, including network partitions [2] and node-level faults (i.e., node crashes and node reboots) [53, 76]. These studies provide invaluable insights for combating the corresponding types of

FTBugs in cloud systems. However, since these studies focus on specific types of triggering faults, their findings may not reflect the characteristics of FTBugs in general.

Barbosa et al. study 28 FTBugs in the Hadoop project to categorize their root causes [7]. Besides only studying a small number of FTBugs, this study also only focuses on root cause classification. To better understand FTBugs in cloud systems, we need to answer important questions such as what faults commonly trigger FTBugs, and what are the relations between the triggering faults and the triggered FTBugs. The answers to these questions can help effectively address FTBugs in cloud systems.

## 2.2   Detecting FTBugs in Cloud Systems

Multiple techniques have been proposed to detect FTBugs. The majority of the proposed techniques [28, 31, 61, 65, 67, 68, 88, 89, 91, 101] detect FTBugs in the error detection and error handling routines. For example, Asiprator [101] detects FTBugs by finding empty or incomplete exception handlers, as well as overly-general handlers that abort the system. As another example, DScope [28] detects FTBugs by identifying loops that do not correctly detect or handle I/O faults and may hang when an I/O operation encounters a corrupted value. These techniques have detected many FTBugs in popular cloud systems [28, 101]. Two proposed techniques [65, 67] also detect FTBugs in the error propagation routines. Specifically, both techniques detect FTBugs by checking whether the error code returned from a callee function is propagated upstream by the caller function.

During the fault tolerance process, besides propagating the error to appropriate components, the accuracy of the propagated error is also important. When the propagated error does not accurately represent the triggering fault, e.g., propagating a file system related error to represent a network partition fault, the required error handling routines may not be activated. However, no existing techniques detect FTBugs that are caused by inaccurate errors.

Several techniques [31, 68] focus on automatically generating error specifications for different functions. Specifically, a generated specification shows the set of values that a function can return on error. This piece of information is critical for the FTBug detection tools that analyze error propagation based on function return values, because these detection tools need to identify error values before checking whether the errors are propagated. However, these specification mining techniques do not differentiate errors triggered by different types of faults. As a result, they can not help detect inaccurate errors. To better detect FTBugs in cloud systems, effective techniques for detecting inaccurate errors are needed.

## 2.3  Exposing FTBugs in Cloud Systems

Some FTBugs are hard to detect statically due to the absence of runtime information. For uncovering these FTBugs, bug exposure techniques can help. Existing FTBug exposure techniques can be mainly classified into two categories: model checking and fault injection testing.

Model checking techniques permute the order of statement executions and fault occurrences to explore all the possible states of a cloud system. Traditionally, model checkers, e.g., TLA+ [69], analyze a model of the cloud system to expose bugs in the system protocols. Recently, *in situ* model checkers are proposed to expose bugs in the cloud system implementations [58, 62, 71, 78, 100]. Since naïvely exploring all possible system states incurs high overhead, these model checkers often employ different strategies to prevent redundant executions. For example, if two node-crashing scenarios will lead to symmetrical recovery behaviors in a cloud system, SAMC [71] will only explore one of the scenarios. As another example, if two network messages are independent, FlyMC [78] will explore only one receiving order of these two messages. However, due to the complexity of real-world cloud systems, model checking a cloud system is still expensive even after pruning out redundant executions.

Fault injection techniques inject faults when testing a cloud system. Various tools are proposed to inject different types of faults. NEAT [2] and Jepson [66] provide mechanisms for injecting network partitions when testing cloud systems, but both tools rely on developers to specify when a network partition starts and stops. Chaos Monkey [81] randomly terminates virtual machines and containers in the specified cluster. CORDS [52] injects file system faults to file I/O operations to check if the faults can be tolerated by the cloud system. PACE [1] crashes multiple nodes at various execution points to test if the cloud system can recover from different persisted file contents after correlated crashes. FCatch [75] injects node crashes to fail writes to shared data so that a later read will get an unexpected value. CrashTuner [77] crashes nodes around accesses to the meta-info variables to expose crash recovery bugs.

Tolerating network partitions is an important problem for cloud systems for two reasons. First, cloud systems run on networked machines where network partitions are inevitable. Second, tolerating network partitions are challenging due to the complexity of these faults. Despite the importance of correctly tolerating network partitions, only two [2, 66] of the existing techniques focus on injecting network partitions to test cloud systems. Moreover, both techniques rely on developers to specify the timing of the network partition. As a result, they are ineffective in exposing the FTBugs whose triggering process has strict timing requirements on the network partition. To thoroughly test how well a cloud system tolerates network partitions, a more systematic approach is needed.

## 2.4 Other Related Work

Other approaches to address FTBugs include preventing FTBugs and fixing FTBugs. One way to prevent FTBugs is to help developers implement correct fault tolerance routines. Along this direction, several programming language features have been proposed to improve the exception mechanism. For example, Harmanci et al. propose abox [63], a Java language extension that allows developers to programatically roll back multiple threads when an exception occurs. The abox feature makes it easier to perform error handling across threads. As another example, Zhang et al. introduce tunneled exceptions [102], a novel mechanism for statically checked exceptions that allows developers to specify when an exception should be checked. This tunneled exception mechanism enables more flexibility in deciding which exceptions should be statically checked, which can help prevent FTBugs in the error detection code.

Automatic bug fixing is an important approach to improve system dependability. Recently, a few techniques are proposed to automatically fix FTBugs. For instance, ErrDoc [92] automatically fixes multiple types of FTBugs including missing error checks, missing error propagation, missing error logging, and missing resource release. However, the accuracy of the generated fixes are still limited. How to automatically generate high quality fixes for more types of FTBugs is an interesting topic for future work.

# Chapter 3: Understanding FTBugs in Cloud Systems

A good understanding of fault tolerance bugs, i.e., FTBugs, in cloud systems is critical for addressing these bugs effectively. Unfortunately, as discussed in §2.1, few existing studies focus on FTBugs in cloud systems. To tackle this problem, this chapter conducts a comprehensive study on bugs in using exception mechanism, a mechanism that is commonly employed for fault tolerance in cloud systems.

## 3.1 Overview

Exception mechanism is widely employed for fault tolerance in cloud systems. At the time of this writing, about 7% of the source code in twelve popular open source cloud systems [44]

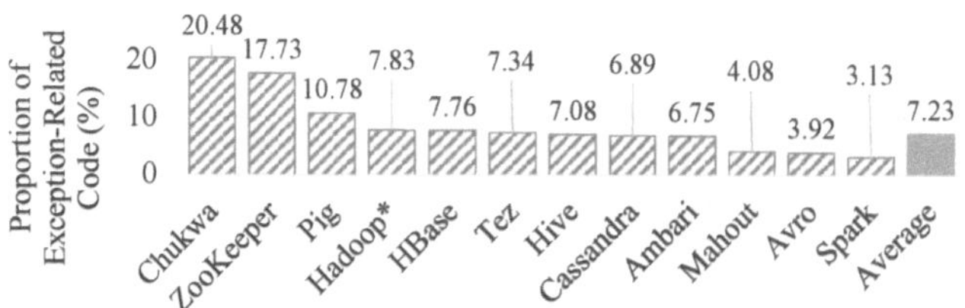



*The Hadoop project includes Hadoop common, Hadoop MapReduce, HDFS, and YARN.

Figure 3.1: Proportion of Source Code (Excluding Empty Lines) that Involves Exception Mechanism in Twelve Cloud Systems.

involve exception mechanism (Figure 3.1), i.e., throwing exceptions, or being enclosed in `try`, `catch`, or `finally` code blocks. Such a widespread use of exception mechanism is mainly due to its advantages over the traditional checking-return-value mechanism [84]. First, it separates the error handling code from main business logic, making programs easier to reason about. Second, the runtime system automatically propagates exceptions up along the call stacks until they are caught, so that errors will not remain unnoticed. Third, it allows developers to combine multiple exceptions by using their common superclass exception, providing greater flexibility for implementing fault tolerance routines.

Unfortunately, the highly diverse environments and the system complexity make exception handling in cloud systems prone to mistakes, which can severely hurt system dependability [59, 101]. When implementing a cloud system, developers need to constantly anticipate various faults that may trigger exceptions. We use *triggering condition* to denote the fault that triggers an exception. Such conditions can either come from the external environment (e.g., a remote node is unreachable), or be caused by internal program states (e.g., a variable is set to a wrong value). Furthermore, the sheer scale of cloud systems (both hardware size and software complexity) dramatically increases the hurdle of correct exception handling. We refer to the mistakes in using exception mechanism as *exception-related bugs*, or *eBugs*.

There are few studies that focus on eBugs in cloud systems. Existing eBug studies in other software systems mainly investigate the root causes based on source code patterns [25, 33, 36, 83], the relation between eBugs and certain language features (e.g., aspect-oriented programming [26] and Android abstractions [36, 83]), and developers' perception on eBugs [33, 83]. Although these studies have discovered useful characteristics of eBugs, none of these studies consider the exception triggering conditions and their relations with eBugs.

These relations are essential for understanding the root causes and facilitating the exposure and the detection of eBugs. Cloud systems often encounter complicated external and internal triggering conditions for exceptions. This unique characteristic motivates us to investigate the root causes of eBugs through understanding their exception triggering conditions.

This chapter presents a comprehensive study on eBugs in cloud systems from the perspective of triggering conditions. In particular, this study covers 210 well-documented eBugs selected from about 5,000 exception-related JIRA [6] issues across six popular open source cloud systems, including Cassandra [39], HBase [46], HDFS [48], Hadoop MapReduce [38], YARN [45], and ZooKeeper [47]. We thoroughly analyze both their bug reports and fixing patches to answer the following key research questions:

- **RQ1**: *How are eBugs triggered in cloud systems?* The answer to this question helps us understand the conditions that trigger eBug-bound exceptions. Our findings can benefit developers to effectively expose eBugs in cloud systems.

- **RQ2**: *What is the relation between the triggering conditions and the root causes of eBugs?* Our in-depth analysis on the root causes and their relations with the triggering conditions can facilitate eBug detection in cloud systems.

- **RQ3**: *What are the impacts of eBugs on cloud systems?* By analyzing the bug impacts, we can understand the severity of eBugs in cloud systems.

To the best of our knowledge, this is the first comprehensive study on eBugs in real-world cloud systems, and the first one from the perspective of triggering conditions. Through this study, we have obtained many interesting findings that open up new research opportunities to combat eBugs in cloud systems. The main findings are: (1) More than half (54%) of the studied eBugs are exposed by non-semantic triggering conditions, most (75%) of which are network faults and file system faults (Finding 1). (2) Most (86%) of the eBugs do not have strong timing requirements on their triggering conditions (Finding 2). (3) 41% of the eBugs are caused by handling an exception in an overly-general (thus incorrect) way. Among them, many (34%) are caused by incorrectly applying the same handling routines to the exceptions that have different types of triggering conditions (Finding 7). (4) 10% of the eBugs are caused by creating exception objects that do not describe their triggering conditions accurately (Findings 3, 4, and 5). (5) Most (74%) of the eBugs affect the dependability of cloud systems, e.g., by crashing nodes or losing data, and developers consider most (82%) of them severe (Finding 8).

These findings show the severity of eBugs in cloud systems, while revealing many new opportunities to combat them. First, we can expose eBugs by simulating non-semantic triggering conditions at simple system states, e.g., consistent global states. Second, we can detect eBugs by analyzing exception triggering conditions. For instance, we can detect inaccurate exceptions by checking whether the exceptions accurately describe their triggering conditions. As another example, we can detect overly-general handlers by examining if the same handling routine is applied to exceptions with different types of triggering conditions.

In summary, this study makes the following key contributions:

- This is the first comprehensive study on eBugs from the perspective of triggering conditions. The study analyzes 210 eBugs that are selected from in six widely-deployed cloud systems.

- This study unveils many interesting findings and explains their implications for addressing eBugs in cloud systems. Specifically, this study finds that triggering conditions provide valuable information for preventing, exposing, and detecting eBugs in cloud systems.

- Through this study, we curate a large benchmark of eBugs in cloud systems. This benchmark can be used to evaluate the effectiveness of the tools that prevent, expose and detect eBugs in cloud systems. The eBug benchmark is available at [20].

## 3.2 Methodology

### 3.2.1 Target Systems

To understand the characteristics of eBugs in real-world cloud systems, we select the target systems based on three criteria: (i) The systems must be diverse to provide an unbiased dataset. (ii) The systems should be mature and popular, so that we can understand the real problems faced by developers. (iii) The systems should be open source and have public issue tracking systems.

With these requirements in mind, we identify the following six cloud systems: (i) Cassandra [39], a highly available peer-to-peer NoSQL database; (ii) HBase [46], a master-slave NoSQL database; (iii) HDFS [48], a distributed file system; (iv) Hadoop MapReduce [38], a distributed data processing framework; (v) YARN [45], a distributed resource management system; and (vi) ZooKeeper [47], a distributed coordination service.

### 3.2.2 EBug Collection

All the target systems use JIRA [6] to manage their issues. Over a time span of more than ten years (from 2007 to 2018), more than 60,000 issues were submitted for these systems. It is time-consuming and impractical to manually inspect all these issues and identify eBugs among them. We therefore apply a few filtering rules to identify the relevant issues.

First, we use the JQL (JIRA Query Language) statement shown in Figure 3.2 to retrieve potentially relevant issues. With this JQL statement, we narrow down all the issues to

```
issuetype = Bug AND status IN (Resolved, Closed)
AND resolution = Fixed AND text ~ "exception*"
```

Figure 3.2: JQL Statement for Retrieving EBug-Related JIRA Issues.

Table 3.1: Investigated Bug Reports in the Studied Systems

| System | Cassandra | HBase | HDFS | MapReduce | YARN | ZooKeeper | Total |
|---|---|---|---|---|---|---|---|
| **Retrieved** | 1,336 | 1,576 | 763 | 460 | 457 | 210 | **4,802** |
| **Studied** | 40 | 92 | 31 | 16 | 23 | 8 | **210** |

only *fully-resolved* (*Resolved* or *Closed* in *status*) and *fixed* bugs whose report contains the keyword *"exception"* or *"exceptions"*. This JQL returns us with 4,802 issues (Row "Retrieved" in Table 3.1).

We further narrow down the retrieved issues by requiring each selected bug report to include a full exception stack trace and a fixing commit. The exception stack trace and the fixing commit are critical for us to fully understand an eBug because they contain information like the exception that is thrown and the root cause of the eBug. We further remove the ones whose root cause is located in test files or non-Java files, because they are not related to the core functionality of the target systems. This leaves us with 1,561 reports.

Finally, we manually inspect the remaining 1,561 reports and keep the ones that are related to exception mechanism as discussed in §3.3. This leaves us with 210 issues for further analysis (Row "Studied" in Table 3.1). We denote an eBug using its bug ID in JIRA, i.e., SYS-###, where SYS is the system name and ### is the eBug's issue ID.

### 3.2.3  EBug Analysis

To answer our three research questions, we perform an in-depth analysis on each eBug based on the bug description (including the exception stack trace), the discussion among developers in the report, and the source code of the target system (including the fix). We also refer to online resources, e.g., documentation, to facilitate our understanding on eBugs. Through this process, we recover the full picture of how each eBug is triggered (RQ1), how the target system incorrectly uses exception mechanism (RQ2), and how each eBug affects the system (RQ3). Then, we classify eBugs according to their triggering conditions, root causes, and bug impacts.

### 3.2.4  Threats to Validity

To maintain the accuracy of our study, we employ different measures to improve our understanding. For example, we use the final fixing commit and sometimes reproduce an eBug to confirm its triggering condition and root cause.

Even though we try to be unbiased, readers need to understand the following limitations of our study. First, all of our subject systems are open source cloud systems. EBugs in commercial cloud systems or other types of software systems may have different characteristics. Additionally, we may miss some eBugs due to our selection process. For example, we may exclude eBugs that do not have full exception stack traces in their bug reports. Finally, we only study eBugs in Java. While the exception mechanism in Java is generally similar to the ones in other languages (e.g., C++, C#, and Python), Java has a few unique features, which may affect developers' practice in using exceptions. Therefore, readers need to be cautious when extending our findings to other scenarios.

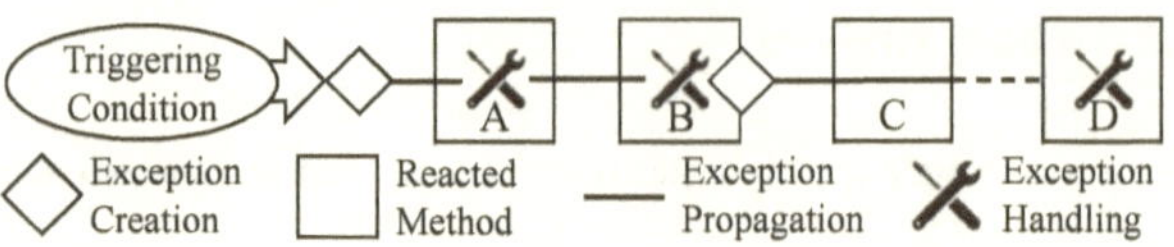


Figure 3.3: The Model of Java's Exception Mechanism.

## 3.3 Exception Mechanism

Figure 3.3 shows the model of Java's exception mechanism. During program execution, an unexpected fault, referred to as a *triggering condition*, occurs. Based on the triggering condition, Java runtime creates and propagates an exception. The *exception propagation* starts from a `throw` statement and ends at a `catch` statement, along the call stack in the reverse call order. After a method catches the exception and performs exception handling (Boxes A, B, and D), it can optionally re-throw the caught exception (Box A), or wrap the caught exception in a new exception before re-throwing it (Box B). Either way, the re-thrown exception starts a new propagation. Along the propagation path, some methods (including the one where the `throw` statement locates) may not catch the exception. Instead, these methods can specify the exception class in the method signatures using the `throws` keyword. In this way, a method notifies its callers that it can propagate the specified exception, so that the callers can implement proper exception handling as needed. Box C represents the scenario where a method does not catch the exception but specifies it in the signature. We consider both catching an exception and specifying an exception in the signature as a method *reacting* to the exception.

```java
void func1(...) throws OtherException {
  try {
    func2(...);
  } catch (SomeException e) {
    someHandling(...);
    throw new OtherException(e);
  }
}
```

Figure 3.4: An Example For Illustrating Java's Exception Mechanism.

Figure 3.4 further illustrates Java's exception mechanism using an example. When method func2() throws a SomeException object, func1() catches and handles the exception (Lines 4–5). At the end of the exception handling, func1() wraps the SomeException in a newly created OtherException object, and throws the new exception at Line 6. func1() also specifies the OtherException (Line 1) so that the callers of func1() can react to the exception accordingly.

We further define the following terms used in our study:

- *Root exception*: Root exception is the exception that is initially created due to a triggering condition. For example, the left-hand side diamond shape in Figure 3.3 represents a root exception.

- *Cause exception*: If an exception object $e_{cause}$ is wrapped by another exception object $e_{wrapper}$, $e_{cause}$ is the cause exception of $e_{wrapper}$. In Figure 3.4, the caught SomeException is the cause exception of the OtherException at Line 6..

- *EBug*: A bug that occurs in creating, throwing, catching, or handling an exception.

## 3.4 Triggering Conditions

The triggering condition is the key to trigger an eBug. In this section, we study both the types of triggering conditions (§3.4.1) and the timing requirements on them (§3.4.2).

### 3.4.1 Triggering Condition Types

We first examine whether the triggering conditions are related to program semantics. Semantic conditions are specific to each individual target system, while findings on non-semantic conditions are general to a broader class of cloud systems. We notice that the majority of the studied eBugs (114 out of 210) are triggered by non-semantic conditions such as a node being unreachable. The remaining eBugs (96 out of 210) are triggered by semantic conditions such as a variable being assigned to an incorrect value.

To better understand non-semantic conditions, we further classify them into the following four categories based on the fault types: (i) *Network fault*: The system encounters a failed network connection. (ii) *File system fault*: The system encounters a failed file system operation, e.g., opening a non-existent file. (iii) *Out of resource*: System resource, such as memory space, is used up. (iv) *Untimely interrupt*: A system interrupt occurs when a thread is sleeping or waiting, e.g., after calling `Thread.sleep()`. Figure 3.5 lists the typical scenarios of each condition type and Table 3.2 shows the detailed distribution of these scenarios.

> **Finding 1**: *Most (75%) of the non-semantic conditions are either network faults or file system faults.*

**Network Fault.** Cloud systems are deployed on network and thereby strive to tolerate network faults. However, network fault is still the most common (40%) type of non-semantic condition in the studied eBugs. With further investigation, we find that most (87%)

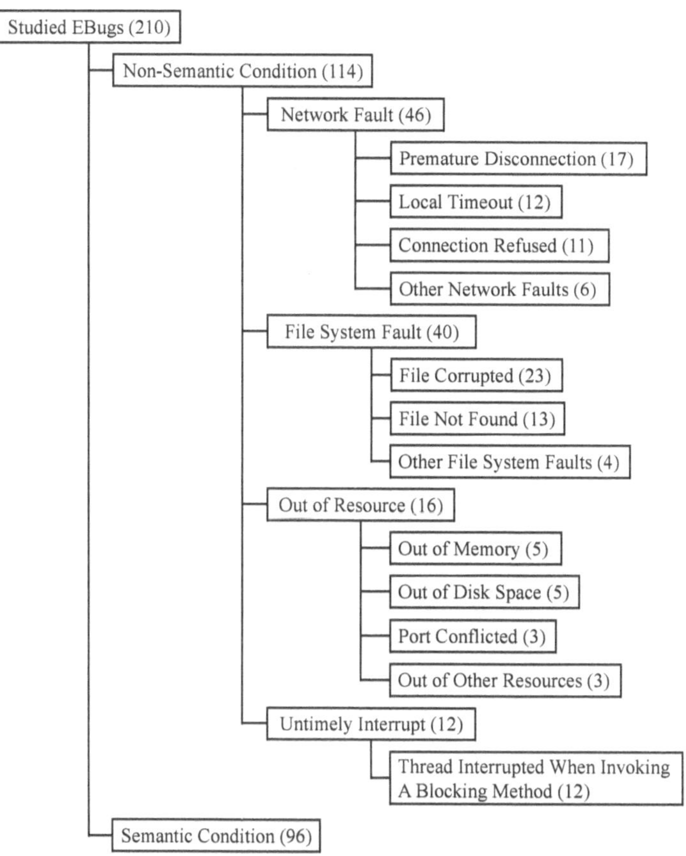


*The numbers in the parentheses show the numbers of the corresponding eBugs.

Figure 3.5: The Triggering Conditions of the Studied EBugs.

Table 3.2: Detailed Distribution of the Triggering Conditions.

| Triggering Condition | CA | HB | HF | MR | YN | ZK | Total |
|---|---|---|---|---|---|---|---|
| Premature disconnection | 0 | 8 | 5 | 1 | 1 | 2 | **17** |
| Local timeout | 2 | 5 | 2 | 0 | 3 | 0 | **12** |
| Connection refused | 1 | 8 | 0 | 1 | 1 | 0 | **11** |
| Other network faults | 0 | 6 | 0 | 0 | 0 | 0 | **6** |
| File corrupted | 10 | 11 | 1 | 1 | 0 | 0 | **23** |
| File not found | 3 | 5 | 3 | 2 | 0 | 0 | **13** |
| Other file system faults | 2 | 0 | 2 | 0 | 0 | 0 | **4** |
| Out of memory | 1 | 2 | 1 | 1 | 0 | 0 | **5** |
| Out of disk space | 1 | 0 | 1 | 1 | 1 | 1 | **5** |
| Port conflicted | 1 | 1 | 1 | 0 | 0 | 0 | **3** |
| Out of other resources | 0 | 0 | 3 | 0 | 0 | 0 | **3** |
| Untimely interrupt | 2 | 1 | 0 | 3 | 6 | 0 | **12** |
| Semantic condition | 17 | 45 | 12 | 6 | 11 | 5 | **96** |
| **Total** | **40** | **92** | **31** | **61** | **23** | **8** | **210** |

**CA**: Cassandra; **HB**: HBase; **HF**: HDFS; **MR**: MapReduce; **YN**: YARN; **ZK**: ZooKeeper;

of the network faults belong to the following three scenarios: (i) *Premature disconnection.* For example, in `HDFS-7009`, a DataNode throws an `EOFException` when a NameNode terminates the connection after sending partial data to the DataNode. (ii) *Local timeout.* For instance, in `HBASE-6299`, an HMaster throws a `SocketTimeoutException` if the HMaster times out before receiving a response from a RegionServer. (iii) *Connection refused.* In `YARN-196`, a NodeMagager tries to connect to a ResourceManager that has not started. As a result, the remote operating system rejects the connection, causing the NodeManager to throw a `ConnectException`. The remaining (13%) network faults are caused by various reasons, such as failed routing and unsuccessful host name resolution.

**File System Fault.** Cloud systems store critical user and system data on file systems. Since file systems are never perfect [54], cloud systems are expected to correctly react to file system faults. For example, when failing to read a data chunk, a distributed file system (e.g., HDFS) may start the data recovery process using a remote data replica. However, we find that a significant number of eBugs are triggered by file system faults. Among these faults, the most frequent scenarios are files being corrupted and files not found: (i) *File corrupted.* For example, in `CASSANDRA-12728`, a Cassandra server throws an `EOFException` when it unexpectedly reads the end of a truncated hint file. (ii) *File not found.* For instance, in `HBASE-9563`, a restarted HMaster throws a `FileNotFoundException` when it fails to find a znode file to read. Other file system faults include access mode violation, file path resolution failure, and disk failure.

**Out of Resource.** Cloud systems interact with system resources extensively. However, the desired resource may not be always available. 14% of the non-semantic eBugs are triggered when certain resource is exhausted. Among the 16 out-of-resource eBugs, 13 are triggered

due to running out of (i) *memory space*, (ii) *disk space*, or (iii) *host ports*. For example, in
`CASSANDRA-11540`, a Cassandra server throws a `BindException` when trying to bind an
occupied port. Other resources include opened file handlers and disk quotas.

**Untimely Interrupt.**  Cloud systems are highly concurrent. They may try to perform two
conflicting operations at the same time. When this happens, one operation may stop the
other via interrupt. We find that, a considerable amount (11%) of non-semantic eBugs are
triggered by untimely interrupts. For example, `YARN-2846` is triggered when one thread of a
NodeManager process is checking the status of a container, while another thread is shutting
down the whole process.

**Semantic Condition.**  About half (46%) of the eBugs are triggered by *semantic conditions*.
Semantic conditions are closely related to program logic, and thereby can be system-specific.
For example, in `CASSANDRA-5725`, a Cassandra server throws an `UnknownColumnFamily-`
`Exception` when it tries to access a nonexistent column family. From this example, we can
see that triggering this type of eBugs needs domain knowledge about the target systems.
For instance, column family is a data structure used in Cassandra to organize both user data
and system data. However, other systems, e.g. HDFS, do not have this concept. Since 46%
of the eBugs are triggered by semantic conditions, they call for more attention from our
communities.

### 3.4.2   Timing Requirements on Triggering Conditions

> **Finding 2**: *Most (86%) of the eBugs do not have strong timing requirements on their triggering conditions.*

Table 3.3: Timing Requirements on EBug Triggering Conditions

| Condition Type | Timing Requirement | | |
|---|---|---|---|
| | **Weak** | **Moderate** | **Strong** |
| Network fault | 9 | 36 | 1 |
| File system fault | 32 | 5 | 3 |
| Out of resource | 5 | 11 | 0 |
| Untimely interrupt | 0 | 10 | 2 |
| Semantic condition | 39 | 34 | 23 |
| **Total** | **85** | **96** | **29** |

EBugs can be triggered only when triggering conditions occur at certain system states. To understand the difficulty of triggering eBugs in cloud systems, we further analyze each eBug's timing requirement on its triggering condition. Similar to a previous bug study in cloud systems [53] we classify the timing requirements into three categories, as shown in Table 3.3.

**Weak Requirement (85 EBugs).** To trigger this type of eBugs, the triggering condition can occur at any consistent global state, or before the system starts. For example, ZOOKEEPER-2757 can be triggered whenever a user issues a delete command with an invalid pathname.

**Moderate Requirement (96 EBugs).** To trigger this type of eBugs, the triggering condition needs to occur on a node when it is in certain states. For example, MAPREDUCE-5251 can be triggered by simulating out of disk space when a reduce task tries to write a map output to disk. There is no need to check the states of other nodes in the system.

**Strong Requirement (29 EBugs).** To trigger this type of eBugs, the triggering condition needs to occur on a node when both the current node and other nodes are in certain states. For example, YARN-3842 can only be triggered when a MapReduce ApplicationMaster requests a NodeManager to start a container, while the NodeManager is still in the initialization phase.

## 3.5  Root Causes

Based on the exception mechanism shown in Figure 3.3, eBugs can be classified into three categories: (i) **Inaccurate exception**, if the eBug is caused by creating an exception object that does not accurately describe the triggering condition; (ii) **Missing reaction**, if the eBug is caused by neither catching nor specifying an exception in the method signature; and (iii) **Incorrect reaction**, if the eBug incorrectly reacts to an exception. Incorrect reaction eBugs can be further broken down into **overly-general reaction**, where different exceptions are incorrectly handled in the same way, and **incorrect reaction logic**, where the reaction logic is incorrect for all exceptions. Figure 3.6 illustrates these four types of eBugs, and Table 3.4 shows their distribution. Note that, previous studies have also classified eBugs based on their

Table 3.4: The Distribution of EBug Root Causes

| Root Cause | EBug # | CA | HB | HF | MR | YN | ZK |
|---|---|---|---|---|---|---|---|
| Inaccurate exception | 21 | 3 | 8 | 4 | 3 | 3 | 0 |
| Missing reaction | 36 | 12 | 11 | 3 | 3 | 4 | 3 |
| Overly-general reaction | 87 | 13 | 42 | 14 | 6 | 11 | 1 |
| Incorrect reaction logic | 66 | 12 | 31 | 10 | 4 | 5 | 4 |
| **Total** | **210** | **40** | **92** | **31** | **16** | **23** | **8** |

**CA**: Cassandra; **HB**: HBase; **HF**: HDFS; **MR**: MapReduce; **YN**: YARN; **ZK**: ZooKeeper;

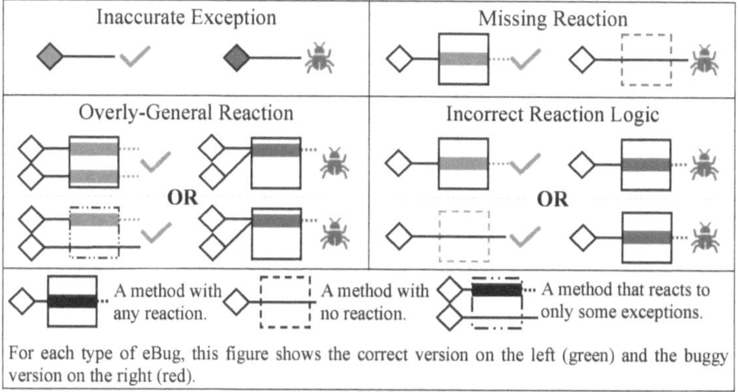


Figure 3.6: Four Types of EBug Root Causes.

root causes [25, 33, 36, 83]. Unlike these studies, our classification focuses on the relation between the triggering conditions and the root causes (RQ2).

## 3.5.1 Inaccurate Exception

Exception objects are expected to accurately represent their triggering conditions so that the system can perform appropriate exception handling. This requires the exception object to instantiate the correct *class* and contain correct information such as an *error message* and a *cause exception*. Table 3.5 shows the number of eBugs where the exception instantiates a wrong class, has a wrong error message, or misses a cause exception.

**Wrong Exception Class**

Exception class is the primary source to indicate the triggering condition. An exception instance with a wrong class will not be handled correctly. We find two ways of creating incorrect exception classes: (i) In five eBugs, the incorrect exception class is the superclass

Table 3.5: The Distribution of Different Types of Inaccurate Exceptions

| Type | Wrong Class | Wrong Message | Lacking Cause | Total |
|---|---|---|---|---|
| EBug # | 13 | 5 | 3 | 21 |

of the intended class. (ii) In the other eight eBugs, the incorrect exception class has no relation with (i.e., neither a superclass nor a subclass of) the intended class.

> **Finding 3**: *Using a superclass of the intended exception makes it difficult to perform correct exception handling.*

We find that `IOException` is the only culprit class in all the five eBugs that use a superclass of the intended exception. For example, in HDFS-8224, a DataNode throws an `IOException` when it tries to read the checksum granularity from a corrupted file. Since other disk failures, e.g., out of disk space, also trigger `IOException`, the DataNode cannot differentiate the exceptions to perform data recovery only for file corruption. To fix this bug, a dedicated subclass exception, `InvalidChecksumSizeException`, is used to denote the case where the file storing the checksum granularity is corrupted.

> **Finding 4**: *In half of the eBugs that create a totally misleading exception, the exception class is inconsistent with its triggering condition.*

When the newly-created class is neither a superclass nor a subclass of the intended one, the exception cannot be correctly caught by its intended `catch` block. Take eBug HBASE-3164 in Figure 3.7 as an example. When a RegionServer opens a META region, it needs to report the update to the RootServer. If the RootServer is currently unreachable, `waitForRootServerConnection()` will return a `null` (Line 2). Instead of throwing an `IOException` that semantically matches the triggering condition (i.e., a network fault),

```
1   void updateMetaLocation() throws IOException {
2     if (waitForRootServerConnection() == null) {
3  -     throw new NullPointerException(...);
4  +     throw new IOException(...);
5     }
6   }
7   void process() {
8     try {
9       updateMetaLocation();
10    } catch (IOException e) {
11      cleanup();
12    }
13  }
```

Figure 3.7: HBASE-3164, an Inaccurate Exception EBug.

the buggy code throws a NullPointerException (Line 3). "We actually throw the NPE [when] it's not an actual NPE", a developer also points out. As a result, even though a proper catch block exists (Lines 10–12), it can not catch the exception to perform appropriate handling operations. Due to this eBug, the META region stays inaccessible.

Among the eight eBugs in this category, four of them are triggered by non-semantic conditions. We find that all the incorrect classes are inconsistent with their conditions (Table 3.6). This makes us wonder: Does each type of non-semantic condition have a set of frequently triggered exception classes? If so, the inconsistency between the frequent classes and the triggered ones may help detect inaccurate exception eBugs.

We analyze all the 114 eBugs with non-semantic triggering conditions. For each eBug, we use the root exception class because it is directly related to the triggering condition. To prevent using the wrong exception classes in the inaccurate exception eBugs, we employ their fixing patches to retrieve the correct exception classes.

Table 3.6: The Triggering Conditions and the Exception Classes of Four EBugs with Wrong Exception Classes

| Bug ID | Triggering Condition | Exception Class |
| --- | --- | --- |
| CASSANDRA-11448 | Out of resource | RuntimeException |
| HBASE-3164 | Network fault | NullPointerException |
| HDFS-2484 | File system fault | LeaseExpiredException |
| YARN-2846 | Untimely interrupt | IOException |

> **Finding 5**: *For non-semantic triggering conditions, a few (1-8) exception classes can cover most eBugs (75-91%).*

As Table 3.7 shows, each condition type triggers only a few exception classes more than once (Column **N**), and these classes cover a majority of eBugs with the corresponding condition type (Column **P**). For example, three exception classes cover 75% of the eBugs that are triggered by an "out of resource" condition. We also notice that these frequently triggered classes do not include the misleading ones shown in Table 3.6. For example, the RuntimeException in CASSANDRA-11448 is not a frequent exception class for the "out of resource" triggering condition.

**Wrong Error Message or Lacking Cause Exception**

When an exception carries a wrong error message, or an exception does not wrap a cause exception, developers may lack critical information about the triggering condition to diagnose the failure. For example, in HDFS-7899, if a DataNode disconnects with an HDFS client, the client will throw an EOFException with a message stating: "Premature EOF: no length prefix available". As the bug reporter points out, this error message "is not very clear to users" because the message does not indicate that the DataNode is unreachable.

Table 3.7: Exception Classes Frequently Triggered by Non-Semantic Triggering Conditions.

| Triggering Condition | N[†] | P[‡] | Top 4 Exception Class (#) |
|---|---|---|---|
| Network fault | 8 | 91% | ConnectException (11)<br>IOException (10)<br>SocketTimeoutException (6)<br>EOFException (5) |
| File system fault | 4 | 78% | EOFException (11)<br>FileNotFoundException (10)<br>IOException (8)<br>IllegalArgumentException (2) |
| Out of resource | 3 | 75% | OutOfMemoryError (5)<br>IOException (4)<br>BindException (3) |
| Untimely interrupt | 1 | 75% | InterruptedException (9) |

[†]Column "N" shows the number of exception classes that are triggered more than once by the corresponding type of triggering conditions. [‡]Column "P" shows the percentage of eBugs with that triggering condition covered by the N classes.

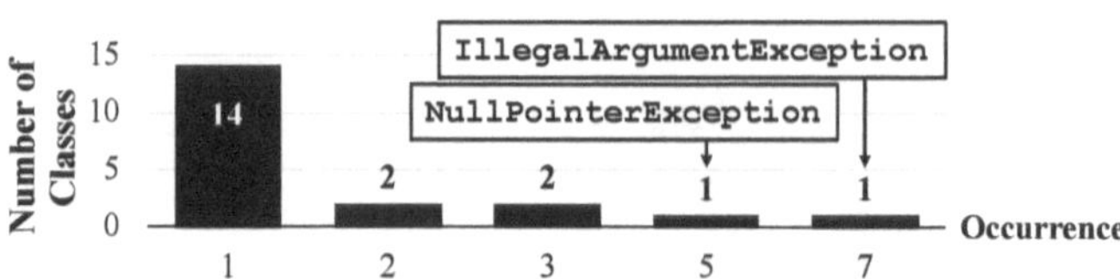


Figure 3.8: Exception Classes Missed by Missing Reaction EBugs.

## 3.5.2 Missing Reaction

Once an exception is thrown, some methods in the call stack need to react to it. If these methods neither catch the exception, nor specify the exception in the method signatures, we refer to this type of mistake as a *missing reaction* eBug. We examine the fixing patch of an eBug to identify which methods should react to an exception. To gain more insights, we also analyze the exception classes that are missed.

> **Finding 6**: *IllegalArgumentException (19%) and NullPointerException (14%) are the most common exception classes that cause missing reactions.*

As shown in Figure 3.8, we find that many exception classes can be missed by developers. Among these classes, `IllegalArgumentException` and `NullPointerException` are more frequent than others. For example, in `CASSANDRA-5701`, a Cassandra server throws an `IllegalArgumentException` when a client queries a nonexistent column family. Since none of the methods in the call stack handles this exception, the Java thread that is serving the request crashes, and the client gets disconnected abruptly.

```
 1    void call() {
 2      try {
 3        reacquireContainer(...);
 4  +     } catch (InterruptedIOException e) {
 5  +     LOG.warn(...);
 6      } catch (IOException e) {
 7        // FileNotFoundException can reach here.
 8        deactivateContainer(...);
 9      }
10    }
11
12    int reacquireContainer(...) throws IOException {...}
```

Figure 3.9: YARN-5103, an Overly-General Reaction EBug.

### 3.5.3  Overly-General Reaction

If a method can throw multiple exception classes, it is a norm for developers to specify only their common parent class in the method signature. For example, method `reacquire-Container()` in Figure 3.9 specifies only an `IOException` (Line 12), but it can throw subclasses like `InterruptedIOException` and `FileNotFoundException`.

However, this common practice poses a big challenge for accurate exception handling, because developers need to be aware of all the potential exceptions that a method can throw. As a result, developers can make overly-general reaction eBugs, i.e., incorrectly handling multiple exceptions in the same way while the exceptions should be treated differently. We find that overly-general reaction causes many (41%) eBugs.

For example, eBug YARN-5103 in Figure 3.9 incorrectly applies the same handling to `IOException` and its subclasses, such as `InterruptedIOException` and `FileNotFound-Exception`. When restarting, a NodeManager will invoke `reacquireContainer()` to

Table 3.8: The Relation between the Triggering Conditions of the Incorrectly Reacted Exception and the Correctly Reacted Exceptions in Overly-General Reaction EBugs

| Relation | Same Type | Different Types | Unknown | Total |
|---|---|---|---|---|
| **EBug #** | 48 | 30 | 9 | **87** |

reload the information of a running container and wait for the container to exit (Line 3). If the NodeManager interrupts the waiting thread because the NodeManager needs to restart again, `reacquireContainer()` will throw an `InterruptedIOException`. The method `call()` incorrectly catches and handles this exception in the same way as other `IOException`s (Lines 6–9). Therefore, the running container stops prematurely for a benign interrupt (Line 8). Instead, the method `call()` should catch the `InterruptedIOException` separately and let the container continue running (Lines 4–5).

> **Finding 7**: *In many (34%) overly-general reaction eBugs, the incorrectly reacted exception and the correctly reacted exceptions are caused by different types of tiggering conditions.*

Although multiple exceptions can be combined and handled in the same way, exceptions triggered by different types of conditions (i.e., network fault, file system fault, out of resource, untimely interrupt, and semantic condition in §3.4.1) may require different handling. We analyze the relation between the correctly reacted exceptions (whose reaction is not changed in the fixing patch) and the incorrectly reacted exception (as specified in the eBug report) in each eBug to see if these exceptions are triggered by different types of conditions (Table 3.8). If the incorrectly reacted exception and the correctly reacted exceptions are triggered by different types of conditions, we label the eBug as *different type*. If the triggering condition types overlap, we label the eBug as *same type*. We cannot infer the triggering conditions

```
1   List<ServerName> fetchServerAddresses() {
2     try {
3       return listServerNames();
4     } catch (KeeperException e) {
5 -     return null;
6 +     return new ArrayList<ServerName>(0);
7     }
8   }
```

Figure 3.10: HBASE-4045, an Incorrect Reaction Logic EBug.

of the correctly handled exceptions in nine eBugs due to insufficient information around the `throw` statements. So, we label them as *unknown*. We observe that, in many (34%) overly-general reaction eBugs, the exceptions are triggered by different types of conditions. For example in YARN-5103 (Figure 3.9), the `InterruptedIOException` is triggered by an untimely interrupt, while other `IOExceptions` are triggered by different types of conditions, like a `FileNotFoundException` triggered by a file system fault.

### 3.5.4 Incorrect Reaction Logic

If a handler is incorrect for all the exceptions it handles, we say that it has *incorrect reaction logic*. Take HBASE-4045 in Figure 3.10 as an example. In HBase, when a RegionServer tries to replicate data to a different cluster, the RegionServer first needs to fetch the names of the target servers from ZooKeeper (Line 3). If ZooKeeper is unreachable, an exception will be thrown. The handler catches the exception and returns a `null` (Lines 4–5). The caller of `fetchServerAddresses()` does not expect the return value to be `null` and dereferences it (not shown in the figure), which crashes the thread. Instead, the handler should return an empty `ArrayList`, which the caller can handle properly. Detecting this type of eBugs requires understanding the system logic, which remains a challenge for future work.

## 3.6  Bug Impacts

We study the eBug impacts from two perspectives. First, we analyze the failure symptoms to understand how eBugs affect cloud systems (Table 3.9). Then, we use the issue priority of each eBug to infer if developers consider the eBug as a severe defect (Table 3.10).

> **Finding 8**: *74% of the eBugs affect the availability (e.g. node downtime) and integrity (e.g., data loss) of cloud systems. Moreover, developers consider most (82%) eBugs as severe defects (i.e., priority not lower than major).*

Overall, eBugs have various failure symptoms. Many of the studied eBugs affect the system availability (e.g., node downtime) and integrity (e.g., data loss). Sometimes, an eBug can turn a transient and benign fault into a severe failure. For example, in `YARN-196`, a NodeManager aborts only because a transient network partition prevents the NodeManager from registering with the ResourceManager. A simple retry fixes the eBug, and allows the NodeManger to start.

We also find that, developers consider most (82%) of the eBugs as severe defects, i.e., having a priority of *blocker*, *critical*, or *major*. Even the seemingly most benign type of symptoms, i.e., *incorrect error message*, can cause much trouble for end users of cloud systems: two thirds of the corresponding issues are assigned with a major or higher priority in JIRA.

Table 3.9: EBug Failure Symptoms

| Symptom | EBug # | CA | HB | HF | MR | YN | ZK |
|---|---|---|---|---|---|---|---|
| Node downtime | 48 | 5 | 25 | 4 | 2 | 7 | 5 |
| Incorrect error message | 44 | 10 | 9 | 13 | 5 | 7 | 0 |
| Data loss or potential data loss | 31 | 5 | 23 | 3 | 0 | 0 | 0 |
| Hang or performance downgrading | 26 | 3 | 12 | 5 | 3 | 2 | 1 |
| Resource leak/exhaustion | 10 | 1 | 3 | 2 | 1 | 1 | 2 |
| Operation failure[†] | 51 | 16 | 20 | 4 | 5 | 6 | 0 |
| **Total** | **210** | **40** | **92** | **31** | **61** | **23** | **8** |

**CA**: Cassandra; **HB**: HBase; **HF**: HDFS; **MR**: MapReduce; **YN**: YARN; **ZK**: ZooKeeper. [†] We only consider an eBug as causing operation failure if it does not have any other symptom.

Table 3.10: JIRA Issue Priority of EBugs

| **Priority** | Blocker | Critical | Major | Minor | Trivial | **Total** |
|---|---|---|---|---|---|---|
| **EBug #** | 21 | 42 | 110 | 33 | 4 | **210** |

# 3.7   Lessons Learned

Our study shows that eBugs seriously affect the dependability of cloud systems (Finding 8). In this section, we discuss implications for existing approaches and opportunities for future research to address eBugs in cloud systems.

## 3.7.1   Testing Cloud Systems under Adversarial Conditions

Software testing is a popular approach for exposing bugs before software release. Many testing techniques have been proposed for exposing software bugs [12, 55, 103], but few are designed for cloud systems [1, 58, 75].

Cloud systems usually run in complex cluster environments, and may encounter different kinds of adversarial conditions, e.g., network faults and file system faults. Improperly handling these conditions can lead to severe consequences. As Figure 3.1 shows, cloud systems often use exception mechanism for fault tolerance. However, Finding 1 indicates that there are issues in tolerating some faults. Existing testing techniques on cloud systems have tried to inject faults like network partitioning [2, 66], file corruption, and out of disk space [52]. However, other adversarial conditions in Figure 3.5, such as connection refused, file not found, port conflicted, and untimely interrupt, have not been attempted in cloud systems. Moreover, researchers and developers can use the triggering conditions summarized in §3.4 as a checklist to test cloud systems. For example, by limiting the available memory and disk space during normal testing, eBugs that are triggered by either "out of memory" or "out of disk space" become more likely to be exposed.

To trigger an eBug, testing tools need to simulate the triggering condition at proper system states. Finding 2 shows that most (86%) eBugs, e.g., ZOOKEEPER-2757 and

`MAPREDUCE-5251`, have a weak or moderate requirement on when the triggering condition should occur. This finding indicates that simple simulation of triggering conditions can expose many eBugs in cloud systems.

### 3.7.2 Preventing EBugs in Cloud Systems

Our findings imply that enhancing exception flow analysis can help prevent eBugs. Exception flow analysis [9, 30, 73, 87, 90] helps developers better understand the exception propagation in the system and thereby better react to exceptions. Throughout our study, we consistently observe that the root causes of many eBugs are related to their exception triggering conditions (Findings 1, 4, 5, and 7). Therefore, by combining exception flow analysis with the related triggering conditions, developers can obtain deeper understanding about what fault triggers an exception, and thus handle the exception correctly. For example, one version of HBase defines 72 exception subclasses that extend `IOException`. For a method handling `IOException`, it will be greatly helpful for preventing overly-general reactions if developers can know each concrete exception and the triggering condition.

### 3.7.3 Detecting EBugs in Cloud Systems

Unlike existing eBug detection tools that focus on empty or incomplete exception handlers [101], overly-general handlers that stop the system [101], missing recovery operations [91], or violations of predefined exception propagation rules [79], our findings (Findings 3, 4, 5, and 7) reveal the important correlation between the root causes and triggering conditions, which suggests new opportunities for detecting eBugs.

Findings 3-5 indicate that inaccurate exceptions do not accurately describe their triggering conditions. Therefore, it is possible to detect these eBugs by checking if the exceptions are consistent with their triggering conditions. In this way, we can detect eBugs like

HBASE-3164, where HBase incorrectly throws a NullPointerException for a network fault. Table 3.7 also provides the commonly triggered exceptions for each non-semantic condition type. Detection tools can use it as a checklist to detect inaccurate exceptions.

Similarly, Finding 7 shows that some overly-general reactions incorrectly apply the same handling routine to the exceptions that are caused by different types of triggering conditions. This suggests a new way to detect overly-general reactions, i.e., by checking if the handled exceptions are triggered by different types of conditions. Using this approach, we can detect eBugs like YARN-5103, where two exceptions (InterruptedIOException and FileNotFoundException) are triggered by different types of conditions (untimely interrupt and file system fault, respectively) but are handled in the same way.

## 3.8  Summary

This chapter presents a comprehensive analysis of 210 eBugs in six popular cloud systems. This is the first eBug study that focus on the exception triggering conditions. The study shows that eBugs affect the availability and the integrity of cloud systems. Therefore, eBugs deserve more attention from multiple communities. The study also reveals many interesting findings that can help address eBugs in cloud systems. Finally, the findings from this study also motivate and inspire the work presented in the following chapters for exposing and detecting FTBugs in cloud systems.

**Chapter 4: Detecting FTBugs in Cloud Systems**

Fault tolerance bugs, i.e., FTBugs, widely exist in cloud systems. Therefore, effective approaches for detecting FTBugs are critical for the dependability of cloud systems. However, as discussed in Chapter 2, some FTBugs have not been addressed by existing bug detection techniques. Specifically, existing techniques do not detect errors that *inaccurately* represent the triggering faults. Moreover, our bug study in Chapter 3 reveals that a non-negligible proportion of exception-related bugs are caused by inaccurate exceptions, i.e., propagating an exception object that is inaccurate for the triggering fault. To address this problem, this chapter proposes DIET and DECAF, two techniques for detecting inaccurate exceptions.

## 4.1  Overview

Various faults can occur in cloud systems. Since different faults have different effects on a cloud system, they often require different fault tolerance routines. For example, transient network partitions may be tolerated by retrying the failed network messages while file corruptions may require copying the data from an intact replica.

Cloud systems decide how to tolerate a fault based on the propagated error. Different errors will be detected by different error detection code and will activate different error handling routines. For example, Figure 4.1 shows the `unassign()` method of HBase's AssignmentManager. When the AssignmentManager tries to close a region on a remote

```
1   class AssignmentManager {
2     void unassign(...) {
3       try {
4         serverManager.sendRegionClose(...);
5       } catch (ConnectException e) {
6         LOG.info(...);
7       } catch (RemoteException e) {
8         master.abort();
9       }
10    }
11  }
```

Figure 4.1: HBase's AssignmentManager Handles Differnt Exceptions Differently.

RegionServer (Line 4), two types of exceptions may be triggered. If the AssignmentManager cannot connect to the RegionServer, a ConnectException will be triggered. In this case, the unassign() method only needs to log the exception (Lines 5–6) and other components of the AssignmentManager will perform the cleanup, e.g., failover the RegionServer (not shown in the figure). However, if the internal state of the remote RegionServer is corrupted, a RemoteException will be triggered. When this happens, the AssignmentManager should abort the HMaster to prevent further damage to the user data (Lines 7–8). As demonstrated by this example, since the propagated error decides which handling routine will be executed, it is important that the propagated error accurately represents the fault.

When an error does not accurately represent its triggering fault, it can affect a cloud system in several ways. First, the dedicated error handling routines may be skipped since the inaccurate error is different from what the error detection code detects. For the example in Figure 4.1, if a ConnectException is thrown when the remote RegionServer is corrupted, the HMaster will not be aborted. Second, unexpected error handling routines may be

```
class DiskAwareRunnable {
  DataDirectory getWriteDirectory(...) {
    directory = getWritableLocation(writeSize);
    if (directory == null) {
-       throw new RuntimeException("Insufficient disk space");
+       throw new IOException(Insufficient disk space");
    }
  }
}
```

Figure 4.2: CASSANDRA-11448, an Inaccurate Exception.

executed since the inaccurate error is detected by unintended error detection code. For the example in Figure 4.1, if a RemoteException is thrown when the AssignmentManager cannot connect to the RegionServer, the HMaster will be accidentally aborted. Finally, when the inaccurate error evolves into a failure, the inaccurate information may mislead the failure diagnosis.

As discussed in §2.2, existing bug detection techniques do not detect errors that are inaccurate. Moreover, our study presented in Chapter 3 shows that a non-negligible proportion of exception-related bugs are caused by inaccurate exceptions, i.e., propagating an exception object that does not accurately represent the triggering fault. As a result, techniques for detecting inaccurate errors are desired. To address this problem, we propose DIET and DECAF, two techniques for detecting inaccurate exceptions.

In cloud systems, an exception object usually has a few *exception features*, such as the exception class and the error message. When an exception object accurately represents its triggering fault, the exception features should convey consistent information about the fault. On the contrary, when the features of an exception object have inconsistent values, the exception is inaccurate. Figure 4.2 shows an inaccurate exception in Cassandra. When there is no enough disk space to serve a write operation (Lines 3-4), the getWriteDirectory() method will throw an exception. The inaccurate exception instantiates class RuntimeException and has an error message saying "insufficient disk space" (Line 5). This exception is inaccurate because the error message implies out of disk space while the exception class implies a general runtime error. A more accurate exception class would be an IOException (Line 6). IOException is more consistent with the error message because it implies that an I/O operation has failed. Motivated by this observation, both of our proposed techniques detect inaccurate exceptions by checking whether an exception has inconsistent feature values.

We first propose a *supervised* technique called DIET. We find that, the class and the error message of an inaccurate exception often imply different *types* of faults. CASSANDRA-11448 in Figure 4.2 is such an example. Based on this observation, DIET detects inaccurate exceptions by checking whether the class and the error message of an exception imply different types of triggering faults. Specifically, DIET is first trained using a collection of exception objects that are labelled with their triggering faults. From this training data, DIET learns the fault types implied by an exception class or an error message. Then, to detect inaccurate exceptions, DIET checks whether the class and the error message of an exception object imply different types of faults. We have implemented a prototype of DIET and applied it to four popular cloud systems including Cassandra, Hadoop, HBase, and ZooKeeper. DIET detects 31 inaccurate exceptions that are never reported before. At the time of this writing, 23 of the detected inaccurate exceptions have been confirmed by developers.

While being effective in detecting inaccurate exceptions, DIET relies on labelled training data. Curating a large collection of labelled exceptions requires substantial manual efforts. To bypass this problem, we propose an *unsupervised* technique called DECAF. We noticed that, when two feature values rarely co-appear on an exception object, the values are likely inconsistent. For example, class `RuntimeException` and error message "insufficient disk space" rarely co-appear on an exception object, and they are inconsistent. Based on this observation, DECAF detects inaccurate exceptions by checking whether the feature values of an exception object rarely co-appear. Specifically, DECAF considers three types of exception features including exception class, error message, and program context. DECAF first analyzes a collection of *unlablled* exception objects to compute how frequently each pair of feature values co-appear. Then, DECAF detects inaccurate exceptions by checking whether an exception object has feature values that rarely co-appear. We have implemented a prototype of DECAF and applied it to the same cloud systems that we used to evaluate DIET. DECAF detects 77 inaccurate exceptions. A comparison of the inaccurate exceptions detected by DIET and DECAF shows that these two techniques are largely complimentary.

Next, we first introduce DIET in §4.2 and then present DECAF in §4.3.

## 4.2  Supervised Detection of Inaccurate Exceptions: DIET

In this section, we present DIET, a supervised technique for detecting inacurate exceptions. The name DIET is the acronym of "**D**etecting **I**naccurate **E**xceptions using **t**riggering condition **T**ypes".

```
1   void updateMetaLocation() throws IOException {
2     if (waitForRootServerConnection() == null) {
3 -       throw new NullPointerException("No server for root");
4 +       throw new IOException("No server for root");
5     }
6   }
```

Figure 4.3: HBASE-3164, an Inaccurate Exception Whose Class and Error Message Imply Different Types of Faults.

## 4.2.1  DIET Idea

DIET is designed based on a simple observation. We find that, when an exception object does not accurately represent the triggering fault, the exception class and the error message often indicate different *types* of triggering faults. Take HBASE-3164 in Figure 4.3 as an example. In this inaccurate exception, the exception class, NullPointerException, implies that a null variable is dereferenced, which is a semantic condition. However, the error message, "no server for root", suggests that the exception is triggered by a network fault. Based on this observation, DIET detects inaccurate exceptions by checking whether the class and the error message of an exception object imply different types of triggering faults.

## 4.2.2  DIET Design

**DIET in A Nut Shell**

Figure 4.4 shows the workflow of DIET. DIET works in two phases: a learning phase and a detection phase. In the learning phase, DIET learns two probabilities from a collection of <Exception, Type> pairs. Each <Exception, Type> pair represents an exception object, "Exception", that is triggered by a fault of type "Type". Figure 4.5 lists a few <Exception, Type> pairs. The first probability learned by DIET is $P(Type|Class)$, i.e., the conditional

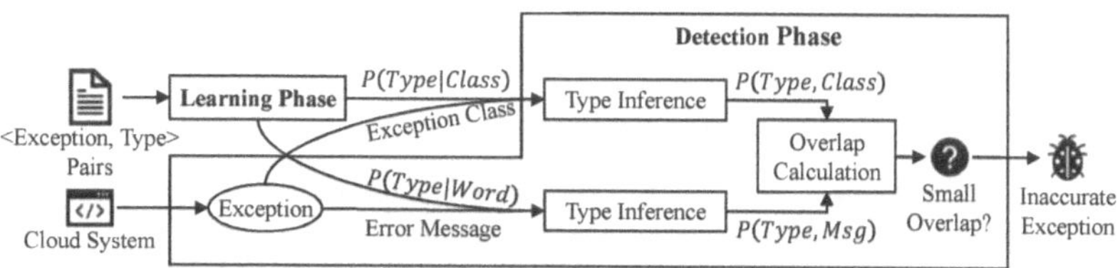

Figure 4.4: DIET's Workflow.

<ConnectException("Connection error."), Network Fault>
<FileNotFoundException("Source file not found."), File System Fault>
<NullPointerException("Key cannot be null."), Semantic Condition>
<IOException("Connection error."), Network Fault>
<IOException("Unable to read from data file."), File System Fault>
...

Figure 4.5: Examples of <Exception, Type> Pairs.

probability of each fault type when the exception instantiates a specific class. This probability indicates the fault type implied by an exception class. The second probability learned by DIET is $P(Type|Word)$, i.e., the conditional probability of each fault type when the exception's error message contains a specific word. This probability indicates the fault type implied by a word in the error message. DIET learns $P(Type|Word)$ instead of $P(Type|Message)$ because different exception objects may have different error messages but words that describe the triggering fault are commonly reused. In the detection phase, DIET analyzes each exception object in a target system, and employs the learned probabilities to infer the triggering fault of an exception object based on the exception class and the error message, respectively. If the class and the error message likely imply different types of triggering faults, DIET reports the exception as inaccurate.

**Learning** $P(Type|Class)$

To learn $P(Type|Class)$, DIET first extracts from each <Exception, Type> pair a <Class, Type> pair, where "Class" and "Type" are the corresponding exception class and fault type. Then, the probability $P(Type|Class)$ for a fault type $t$ and an exception class $c$ is computed using the following equation:

$$P(t|c) = \frac{\text{number of <Class, Type> where Class=}c\text{ and Type=}t}{\text{number of <Class, Type> where Class=}c} \tag{4.1}$$

**Learning** $P(Type|Word)$

To learn $P(Type|Word)$, DIET first extracts from each <Exception, Type> pair a <Message, Type> pair, where "Message" and "Type" are the corresponding error message and fault type. For each <Message, Type> pair, DIET further extracts one or more <Word, Type> pairs, where each extracted "Word" is a case-insensitively unique keyword in "Message". DIET considers keywords to be the words that correlate with the triggering fault. As a result, numbers, conjunctions, determiners, and adverbs are not keywords. For instance, the error message in Figure 4.3, "No server for ROOT", contains two keywords, "server" and "root". Finally, the probability $P(Type|Word)$ for a fault type $t$ and a word $w$ is computed using the following equation:

$$P(t|w) = \frac{\text{number of <Word, Type> where Word=}w\text{ and Type=}t}{\text{number of <Word, Type> where Word=}w} \tag{4.2}$$

**Detecting Inaccurate Exceptions**

In the detection phase, DIET detects inaccurate exceptions by checking whether the class and the error message of an exception imply different types of triggering faults.

```
1  // The exception object to be analyzed
2  IOException("An I/O fault occurs");
```

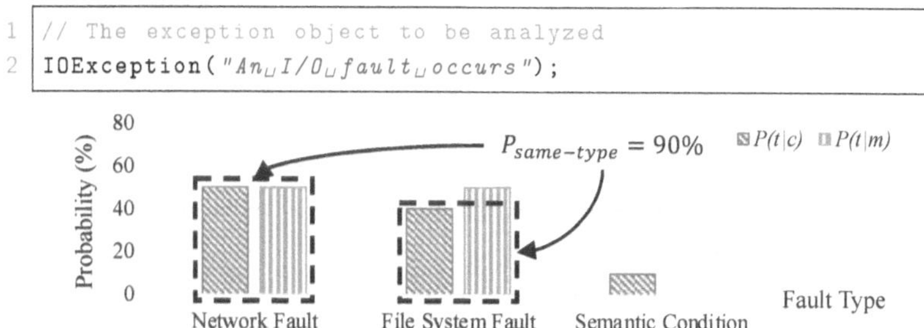


Figure 4.6: An Example of the Calculation of $P_{same-type}$.

For each exception to analyze, DIET first extracts the exception class $c$ and looks up the learned probability $P(t|c)$ for each fault type $t$. $P(t|c)$ is the likelihood that exception class $c$ implies fault type $t$. Then, DIET extracts the error message $m$ and the unique keywords $w_1$–$w_n$. For each keyword $w_i$, DIET looks up the learned probability $P(t|w_i)$ for each fault type $t$. $P(t|w_i)$ is the likelihood that the keyword $w_i$ implies fault type $t$. Next, DIET computes the probability of each fault type given the whole error message $m$ by averaging $P(t|w_i)$ for all the keywords $w_1$–$w_n$ in the error message:

$$P(t|m) = \frac{\sum_{i=1}^{n} P(t|w_i)}{n} \tag{4.3}$$

Afterwards, DIET uses $P(t|c)$ and $P(t|m)$ to compute how likely exception class $c$ and the error message $m$ imply the same type of faults. We use $P_{same-type}$ to denote this likelihood. A straightforward approach is to use the following equation to compute the statistical likelihood:

$$P_{same-type} = \sum_{t \in \text{Fault Types}} [P(t|c) \times P(t|m)] \tag{4.4}$$

However, this equation cannot handle the case in which both the exception class and the error message imply a general condition that includes multiple types of faults. The exception in Figure 4.6 is such an example. This exception instantiates class `IOException` and has an error message, "an I/O fault occurs". Since both the class and the message imply an I/O fault, they are consistent. However, since both network operations and file system operations can encounter I/O faults, class `IOException` can have high probabilities of implying a network fault and a file system fault, respectively. Similarly for the error message, "an I/O fault occurs". If the distributions of $P(t|c)$ and $P(t|m)$ are as shown in the figure, Equation 4.4 will compute $P_{same-type}$ as only 45%, which does not reflect that the class and the message are consistent. To address this problem, DIET uses the "overlap" of $P(t|c)$ and $P(t|m)$ to indicate how likely class $c$ and message $m$ imply the same type of fault. Specifically, the overlap is calculated using the following equation:

$$P_{same-type} = \sum_{t \in \text{Fault Types}} \min(P(t|c), P(t|m)) \tag{4.5}$$

The dashed boxes in Figure 4.6 illustrates how Equation 4.5 computes $P_{same-type}$. Intuitively, $P_{same-type}$ reflects the similarity between $P(t|c)$ and $P(t|m)$. The greater $P_{same-type}$ is, the more consistent class $c$ and message $m$ are. Finally, if the $P_{same-type}$ of an exception is smaller than a configurable threshold, DIET will report the exception as inaccurate.

### 4.2.3  DIET Implementation

We implement a prototype of DIET to detect inaccurate exceptions in Java-based cloud systems. However, DIET's idea can also be applied to systems implemented in other programming languages as long as the exception mechanism supports exception class and error message. We now discuss DIET's implementation details, especially how DIET extracts exception objects in the detection phase.

**Identifying Exception Objects.** Given a cloud system to analyze, DIET extracts exception objects from the source code by identifying "`throw new ...;`" statements. This is the programming convention of creating and throwing an exception object.

**Identifying Exception Classes and Error Messages.** For each identified exception object, DIET needs to extract the exception class and the error message to analyze. DIET uses the class instantiated by the new statement as the exception class. To identify the error message, DIET extracts the string constants used inside the new statement. Since developers usually hard-code most of the error message inside an exception instantiation statement, DIET can correctly identify most error messages using this heuristic.

**Pruning Non-Root Exceptions.** Among the extracted exception objects, DIET only analyzes root exceptions that carry error messages. Recall that a root exception does not contain any cause exception (§3.3). DIET focuses on root exceptions because they usually describe the triggering faults more accurately than their wrapper exceptions. To identify root exceptions, DIET checks whether the last parameter of the exception instantiation is a variable named t, e, or e with a number (e.g., e1). These are the common variable names for the cause exception.

### 4.2.4 DIET Evaluation

**Methodology**

To evaluate the effectivenss of DIET, we apply DIET to real-world cloud systems and check the number of inaccurate exceptions detected by DIET. Specifically, we choose

Table 4.1: Applying DIET to Real-World Cloud Systems

| System (Version) | Cassandra (3.11.5) | Hadoop[†] (3.1.2) | HBase (2.1.4) | ZooKeeper (2.4.14) | Total |
|---|---|---|---|---|---|
| Throw Statement | 2,823 | 9,853 | 5,020 | 429 | **18,125** |
| Root with Message | 1,282 | 3,090 | 1,374 | 159 | **5,905** |
| Calculated Exception | 550 | 1,579 | 716 | 84 | **2,929** |
| Reported Exception | 100 | 136 | 73 | 5 | **314** |
| Candidate | 9 | 20 | 2 | 0 | **31** |

[†] Hadoop includes Hadoop common, HDFS, MapReduce, and YARN.

the latest versions (at the time of this writing) of four popular cloud systems, including Cassandra-3.11.5, Hadoop-3.1.2, HBase-2.1.4, and ZooKeeper-2.4.14.

To train DIET, we curate a collection of <Exception, Type> pairs using the root exceptions extracted from the 210 exception-related bugs (i.e., eBugs) studied in Chapter 3. Specifically, we identify the root exception and the triggering condition in each eBug. For inaccurate exception eBugs, we use the exception object in the fixed code since the exception object in the buggy code does not accurately represent the triggering fault. Among the 210 eBugs, we identify 166 <Exception, Type> pairs because the exception object in the remaining 44 eBugs do not have an error message.

It is worth noting that, since we train DIET using the exception objects curated from the eBug study, the fault types considered by DIET are the five types of triggering conditions identified in the study, i.e., network fault, file system fault, out of resource, untimely interrupt, and semantic condition. Developers can use the fault types that are suitable for their cloud systems.

**Evaluation Result**

Table 4.1 gives an overview of DIET's analysis. From the target cloud systems, DIET extracts 18,125 throw statements (Row "Throw Statement"). 5,905 of these statements are throwing a root exception with an error message (Row "Root with Message"). DIET manages to calculate the $P_{same-type}$ of 2,929 exceptions using Equation 4.5 (Row "Calculated Exception"). If an exception has a $P_{same-type} \leq 0.2$ (an empirically-chosen threshold value), DIET will report the exception as inaccurate. Finally, DIET reports 314 inaccurate exceptions (Row "Reported Exception"). We inspected all the reports, and identified 31 candidates for real inaccurate exceptions (Row "Candidate"). Note that, DIET fails to calculate the $P_{same-type}$ score for half of the root exceptions with error messages, and DIET's false positive rate is high (283 out of 314 reported exceptions). This is mainly because we only use a small dataset (166 <Exception, Type> pairs) to train DIET, and many exception classes and message keywords in our experimental subjects are not included in the training data. This can be improved by training DIET with a larger dataset.

Among the 31 candidates, we found two eBugs in which the inaccurate exceptions can cause failure symptoms. The remaining 29 candidates are bad practices. A bad practice is an inaccurate exception whose class and error message are indeed inconsistent, but the exception has not caused failure symptoms. However, a bad practice may introduce eBugs in the future because it is difficult to correctly handle an inaccurate exception. For example, since the exceptions in eBug HDFS-8224 and HBASE-3164 are inaccurate, when developers implemented the corresponding exception handlers later, the exceptions were not handled properly.

We report all these bugs and bad practices to developers of these cloud systems. So far, developers have confirmed the two eBugs and 21 bad practices (Table 4.2). More

Table 4.2: Bugs and Bad Practices Detected by DIET

| System | Bug | Bad Practice | | |
|---|---|---|---|---|
| | Confirmed | Confirmed | Pending | Rejected |
| Cassandra | 0 | 8* | 1 | 0 |
| Hadoop | 2 (1 fixed) | 13 (9 fixed) | 2 | 3 |
| HBase | 0 | 0 | 0 | 2 |
| ZooKeeper | 0 | 0 | 0 | 0 |
| **Total** | **2 (1 fixed)** | **21 (9 fixed)** | **3** | **5** |

*Cassandra developers will fix six out of eight confirmed bad practices in the next major update.

importantly, all of these 23 confirmed issues are "previously unknown". At the time of this writing, developers have fixed 10 issues, and will fix another six issues in next major updates.

**EBugs.** DIET detects two eBugs, which are both confirmed by the developers. Both inaccurate exceptions are caused by using incorrect classes. For example, in one of them, `HADOOP-16295`, a DataNode throws an `IOException` when it is interrupted during file renaming. This leads to a checking of disk health, which is necessary only when the `IOException` is triggered by a file system error, e.g., when the renaming actually fails. These eBugs highlight the importance of throwing exceptions with accurate classes. When the exception class does not match its triggering condition, the system may misbehave in two ways. First, the unintended handling operations may be executed, such as both bugs found by DIET. Second, the intended handling operations may be skipped. Although DIET has not found any new bugs with this symptom, they do exist in real-world cloud systems, e.g., `CASSANDRA-11448`.

**Bad Practices.** DIET detects 29 bad practices. 21 of these bad practices have been confirmed by developers. Although these bad practices have not caused any failure symptoms, developers act proactively to these reported bad practices. For example, Hadoop developers have fixed nine out of thirteen confirmed bad practices [19], and Cassandra developers will fix six out of eight confirmed bad practices in Cassandra's next major update [13–17]. Developers rejected five bad practices, because they believed that these reported candidates work as intended. For example, in HBase, a `RuntimeException` is used to represent a file system error. Developers thought it is a norm in HBase to use `RuntimeException` for a fatal file system error [18].

### 4.2.5 Discussion

While being effective in detecting inaccurate exceptions, DIET needs to be trained using a collection of labelled exceptions. Moreover, as Table 4.1 shows, the quality (both in size and in diversity) of this training data will affect DIET's effectiveness. However, curating a high quality training data requires substantial manual effort. To bypass this problem, we propose DECAF, an unsupervised technique for detecting inaccurate exceptions.

## 4.3 Unsupervised Detection of Inaccurate Exceptions: DE-CAF

This section presents DECAF, our unsupervised technique for detecting inaccurate exceptions. The name DECAF is the acronym of **D**etecting inaccurate **E**xceptions using **C**o-**A**ppearance **F**requency.

```
1   // An exception whose class and message are inconsistent.
2   NullPointerException("Connection␣error.");
3
4   // Other exceptions that instantiate NullPointerException.
5   NullPointerException("Key␣cannot␣be␣null.");
6   NullPointerException("Handler␣returned␣null.");
7   NullPointerException("Identifier␣cannot␣be␣null.");
8   ...
9
10  // Other exceptions with message "connection error".
11  ConnectException("Connection␣error.");
12  IOException("Connection␣error.");
13  EOFException("Connection␣error.");
14  ...
```

Figure 4.7: Inconsistent Exception Feature Values Rarely Co-Appear.

### 4.3.1  DECAF Idea

As discussed in §4.1, the problem of detecting inaccurate exceptions can be addressed through detecting exceptions that have inconsistent feature values. To detect inconsistent feature values without learning from a labelled data set, DECAF exploits the following observation: *Two feature values that rarely co-appear on an exception object are likely inconsistent.* For example, Line 2 in Figure 4.7 shows an exception whose class, NullPointerException, and error message, "connection error", are inconsistent. At the same time, the class, NullPointerException, and the message, "connection error", rarely co-appear on an exception. In other words, an exception instantiating NullPointerException rarely has an error message saying "connection error" (Lines 4–8),

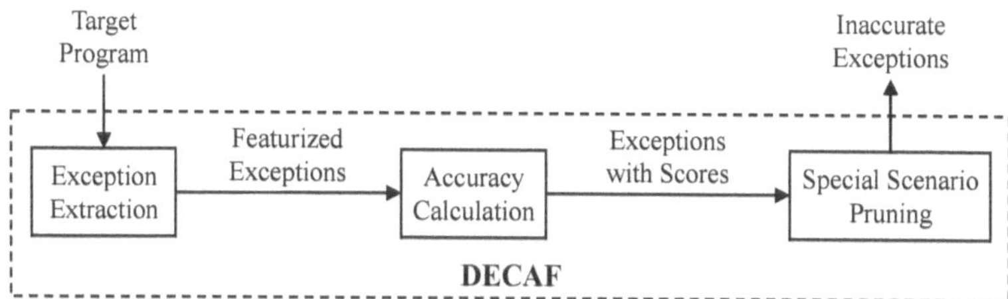


Figure 4.8: The Workflow of DECAF.

and an exception whose message is "connection error" rarely instantiates NullPointer-Exception (Lines 10–14). Based on this observation, DECAF detects inaccurate exceptions by checking whether the feature values of an exception rarely co-appear.

## 4.3.2 DECAF Design

**DECAF in A Nut Shell**

Figure 4.8 shows the workflow of DECAF. To detect inaccurate exceptions in a target system, DECAF first extracts all the exception objects and their exception features from the system's source code. Then, DECAF computes an accuracy score for each exception based on how frequently the exception's feature values co-appear. In two special scenarios, rarely co-appearing values do not indicate that the exception object is inaccurate. The first scenario is when the use of the rarely co-appearing features follows a programming convention. The second scenario is when one of the feature values is not correlated with any fault so there is no frequently co-appearing value. DECAF further prunes out exceptions that belong to these two scenarios before reporting inaccurate exceptions. When reporting inaccurate exceptions, DECAF ranks the exception objects from the most inaccurate to

```
class FileManager {
  void openFile(...) {
    try{
      ...
    } catch (IOException e) {
      if (file == null) {
        throw new RuntimeException("File does not exist.");
      }
    }
    ...
  }
}
```

Figure 4.9: An Inaccurate Exception whose Error Message is Consistent with the Program Context.

the least inaccurate. Developers can decide the number of exception objects to analyze according to the test budget.

**Extracting Features**

DECAF analyzes the consistency of three exception features: *exception class*, *error message*, and *program context*. DECAF considers the class and the error message of an exception object because developers usually encode information about the triggering fault in these features. Since the program context reflects what the system is doing when the exception is triggered, the program context also correlates with the triggering fault. For instance, a file system fault usually happens when the system is interacting with a file system. Moreover, by checking the consistency between an exception class and a program context, DECAF can detect inaccurate exception classes even in the absense of error messages.

To be more specific, the exception class feature is the class instantiated by the exception object. The error message feature is represented by the set of case-insensitively unique keywords in the exception's error message. DECAF maintains a list of words that convey little information about triggering faults, e.g., numbers, conjunctions, determiners, and adverbs. Words outside of this list is considered as keywords. For example, the error message feature of the exception in Figure 4.9 is {"file", "exist"}.

To represent the program context feature, DECAF considers the following five elements in the program context: the *class* and the *method* inside which the exception object is created, the *branch condition* if the exception object is created within a `if-else` branch, the *case identifier* if the exception object is created within a `switch-case` clause, and the *caught exception class* if the exception is created inside a `catch` clause. Specifically, the program context feature is represented using the caught exception class and the set of case-insensitively unique keywords in the other four program context elements.

To extract the keywords from the four program context elements, DECAF first breaks down each programming language identifier in the elements into natural language words. For example, method name "`openFile()`" will be broken down into words "open" and "file". Then, DECAF collects the unique keywords from the extracted natural language words. DECAF considers natural language words instead of programming language identifiers because different identifiers that consist of similar words usually refer to similar contexts, e.g., `openFile()` and `open_file()`. DECAF does not break down the caught exception class because different exception classes usually represent different triggering faults. Finally, DECAF combines the keywords and the caught exception class to form the program context feature. For example, the program context feature of the exception in Figure 4.9 is {"file", "manager", "open", "IOException", "null"}.

**Evaluating The Accuracy of An Exception**

After extracting the exception objects and their exception features from a target program, DECAF computes an accuracy score for each exception object based on the consistency of the exception features. Let us look at an example to understand how the accuracy score should be computed. Figure 4.9 shows an exception being thrown when the program tries to open a nonexistent file. This exception is inaccurate because the exception class, `RuntimeException`, does not indicate that the file to be opened does not exist. Instead, the exception should instantiate `FileNotFoundException`, which accurately describes the triggering fault. As can be seen from this example, even if the error message and the program context are consistent, this exception is inaccurate because the exception class, `RuntimeException`, is inconsistent with the program context (and the error message). In other words, an exception object is inaccurate as long as a pair of exception features are inconsistent. As a result, DECAF computes the accuracy of an exception object based on the most inconsistent feature pair. Formally, DECAF computes the accuracy of an exception object using the following equation:

$$
\begin{aligned}
Accuracy(exception) = Min(&Consistency(exception.class, exception.message), \\
&Consistency(exception.class, exception.context), \quad (4.6) \\
&Consistency(exception.message, exception.context))
\end{aligned}
$$

Note that error message is an optional exception feature. When an exception object does not have an error message, its accuracy is determined by the consistency between the exception class and the program context. To handle this scenario, function *Consistency*() will return the maximum value when one of its parameters is `null` (representing the absence of an error message). Next, we discuss the details of *Consitency*(), i.e., how DECAF computes the consistency of two feature values based on how frequent the two values co-appear.

**Computing the Consistency of Two Feature Values**

To compute the consistency of two feature values, DECAF checks how frequently the two values co-appear. The more frequently two values co-appear, the more consistent these values are.

The frequency of the co-appearance can be measured using the confidence of the values' association rules [97]. Specifically, for two feature values, $val_a$ and $val_b$, there are two association rules. The first rule, "$\{val_a\} \implies \{val_b\}$" dictates that when $val_a$ appears on an exception object, so does $val_b$. On the contrary, the second rule, "$\{val_b\} \implies \{val_a\}$" dictates that when $val_b$ appears on an exception object, so does $val_a$. The confidence of an association rule measures how frequently the rule is true. The confidence is computed using the following equation:

$$Conf(\{val_i\} \implies \{val_j\}) = \frac{|\{\text{exceptions which both } val_i \text{ and } val_j \text{ appear on}\}|}{|\{\text{exceptions which } val_i \text{ appears on}\}|} \quad (4.7)$$

The higher the confidence is, the more frequent an association rule is true.

When both rules have high confidence scores, the two feature values frequently co-appear. Therefore, the values are consistent. Visually, if we use $set_a$ to denote the exceptions that $val_a$ appears on, and use $set_b$ to denote the exceptions that $val_b$ appears on, this is the case in which the two sets are largely overlapped, as represented by the left-hand scenario in Figure 4.10. On the contrary, if both rules have low confidence scores, the two sets have little overlap, as shown by the middle scenario in the figure. In this case, since the two feature values rarely co-appear, they are inconsistent. It is also possible that one rule has

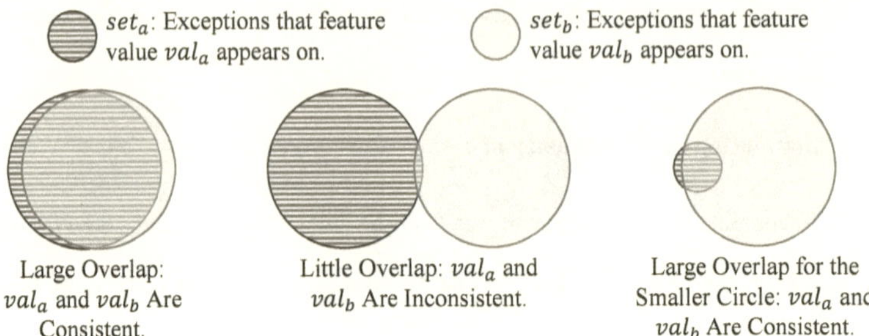


Figure 4.10: Measuring Feature Consistency.

a high confidence score while the other rule has a low confidence score, as represented by the right-hand scenario in the figure. In this case, the value with a smaller set, i.e., $val_a$, likely indicates a sub-type fault of what the other value indicates. For example, $val_a$ implies the "file not found" condition, while $val_b$ implies a file system fault. Therefore, two feature values should be considered as consistent. Integrating these three scenarios, DECAF computes the feature consistency using the following equation:

$$Consistency(val_a, val_b) = Max(Conf(\{val_a\} \implies \{val_b\}), Conf(\{val_b\} \implies \{val_a\}))$$

$$(4.8)$$

**Determining the Appearance of A Feature Value**

Since DECAF computes feature consistency based on how frequently two feature values co-appear, we need to define the *appearence* of a feature value.

It is straightforward to define the appearance of an exception class. If an exception object, *ex*, directly instantiates a class, *cls*, i.e., not through instantiating a subclass of *cls*, then *cls* appears on *ex*.

For error message and program context, defining the appearance of a feature value is trickier, because a value of these features is a set instead of a single class name. One naïve approach is to consider a value, *val*, as appearing on *ex* only when *ex*'s corresponding feature value contains *all* the elements in *val*. For example, if *ex*'s error message feature value is {"file", "exist"}, then another error message feature value, {"file", "read"}, does not appear on *ex*. However, this approach will limit the number of exception objects that a feature value appears on, because error messages and program contexts can have keywords that infrequently used in the system. As a result, even inconsistent value pair can have a high consistency score. Take Figure 4.9 as an example. Exception class `RuntimeException` and error message "file does not exist" are inconsistent. However, they can have a high consistency score if this is the only exception whose error message contains keywords "file" and "exist". Even if many other exceptions whose error message contains keyword "file" do not instantiate `RuntimeException`, these exceptions will not affect the consisency score of class `RuntimeException` and message "file does not exist".

Instead, DECAF considers *val* as appearing on *ex* if *ex*'s corresponding feature value contains *any* of *val*'s elements. Using the same example above, if *ex*'s error message feature value is {"file", "exist"}, then the other error message feature value, {"file", "read"}, appears on *ex*.

**Pruning Special Scenarios**

After computing the accuracy score of each exception object based on the most inconsistent feature pair, DECAF ranks the exceptions according to their scores. Normally, the lower the

```
1  class NodeProbe {
2    Object getColumnFamilyMetric(..., String metricName) {
3      switch (metricName) {
4        ...
5        default:
6          throw new RuntimeException("Unknown table metric");
7      }
8    }
9  }
```

Figure 4.11: An Exception Object that Has Inconsistent Features but Follows a Programming Convention.

accuracy score, the more inaccurate the exception object. However, there are two scenarios in which a low accuracy score does not imply an inaccurate exception. The first scenario is when the use of the inconsistent feature value pair follows a programming convention. The second scenario is when one of the inconsistent feature values is not correlated with any fault, so there is no frequently co-appearing feature value. DECAF further prunes out exception objects that belong to these two scenarios before reporting inaccurate exceptions.

To determine whether the use of a feature value pair follows a programming convention, DECAF counts the number of exception objects on which the two values co-appear. If the number exceeds a configurable threshold, DECAF considers the use of the value pair as following a programming convention. In the rest of this section, we use $N_{convention}$ to denote this threshold.

Figure 4.11 shows an exception object in Cassandra that belongs to this scenario. In this example, method getColumnFamilyMetric() will throw an exception if the metric to query is invalid. DECAF computes a low accuracy score for this exception because the exception class, RuntimeException, rarely co-appears with the message feature, {"table",

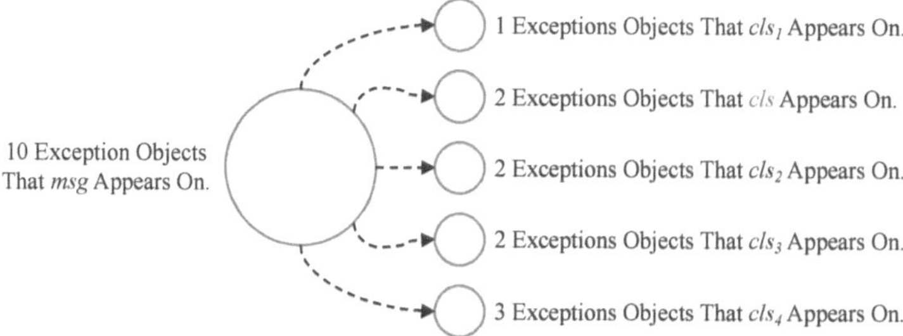



Figure 4.12: An Example in which Exception Class *cls* Is Inconsistent with Error Message *msg*, and *msg* Has No Frequently Co-Appearing Exception Class.

"metric"}. Usually, when an exception's error message contains one of these keywords, the exception is triggered by an invalid user request. Therefore, these keywords frequently co-appear with class `InvalidRequestException`. However, when the invalid query tries to access nonexistent data, such as the nonexistent table metric in this example, the triggered exception will instantiate `RuntimeException`. Specifically, in the Cassandra version analyzed by DECAF, there are 282 exception objects whose error message contains one of these keywords. 159 of these exceptions instantiate `InvalidRequestException`. However, another 23 of these 282 exception objects instantiate `RuntimeException`. If $N_{convention}$ is configured smaller than 23, DECAF will remove this exception from inaccurate exception candidates.

To determine whether a feature value frequently co-appears with any other values, DECAF compares the co-appearance frequencies of each value pair. Specifically, when feature value $val_a$ is inconsistent with feature value $val_b$, and DECAF wants to determine whether $val_b$ has any frequently co-appearing value, DECAF will check every value in $val_a$'s feature to see how frequently that value co-appears with $val_b$. If no value co-appears with

$val_b$ $N_{freq}$ (a configurable threshold) times as frequently as $val_a$ does, DECAF considers $val_b$ as having no frequently co-appearing values. Take Figure 4.12 as an example. In this case, exception class *cls* is inconsistent with error message *msg*, and DECAF wants to determine whether *msg* has any frequently co-appearing exception classes. If $N_{freq}$ is greater than 1.5, DECAF will consider *msg* as having no frequently co-appearing exception class, because there is no exception class that co-appears with *msg* $N_{freq}$ times as frequently as *cls* does.

### 4.3.3  DECAF Implementation

We implement a prototype of DECAF to detect inaccurate exceptions in cloud systems. DECAF also focuses on Java-based cloud systems so that we can compare DECAF with DIET. We now further explain the implementation details of DECAF.

**Pruning Test-Related Code**

When extracting exception objects from a target system, DECAF ignores the code for testing the system. Since test-related code and the system's core functionality may follow different programming conventions, analyzing the core functionality and the test code together may affect DECAF's accuracy in identifying inconsistent feature values. DECAF identifies test-related code by checking the path names of the Java files. If a path name contains the word "test" (case insensitive), DECAF considers the code in the corresponding file as test-related.

**Identifying Exception Objects**

After pruning the test-related code, DECAF extracts exception objects from the remaining source code. Specifically, DECAF identifies exception objects through identifying the new statements that instantiates an exception class. DECAF identifies exceptions classes by checking whether the class name ends with word "Exception", "Error", or "Throwable". In practice, it is a convention to end an exception class name with one of these keywords.

**Extracting Error Messages**

For each identified exception object, DECAF will try to extract the error message carried by the object. According to the programming convention, DECAF assumes that the error message is the first parameter in the exception instantiation, i.e., the new statement.

DECAF recognizes three types of error message. The first type of error message consists of a single string constant. DECAF identifies these messages by checking whether the first parameter of an exception instantiation is a string constant.

The second type of error message is the concatenation of multiple string constants, variables, and function invocations. DECAF identifies these messages by checking whether the first parameter of an exception instantiation is a summation that involves at least one string constant. If so, DECAF extracts the string constants and all the programming language identifiers (i.e., variable names and function names) in the first parameter to form the error message. The identifiers will be further broken down into natural language words before integrated into the error message feature. The breakdown process will be explained later.

The last type of error message is constructed through calling `String.format()`, a string formatng method provided by Java. DECAF identifies these messages by checking whether the first parameter of an exception instantiation is an invocation of `String.format()`. If so, according to the API rules of `String.format()`, DECAF extracts the string constants from the first parameter of `String.format()` and the identifiers from the remaining paramaters to construct the error message. These identifiers will also be broken down into natural language words before integrated into the error message feature.

**Breaking Down Programming Language Identifiers**

To break a programming language identifier into natural language words, DECAF exploits the programming conventions for constructing these identifiers. First, DECAF cuts the identifier at numbers and underscores ("_") to break the identifier into a list of consecutive letters. For example, DECAF will break identifier "`read_file`" into words "read" and "file". Underscores are commonly used to combine words into an identifier. Moreover, underscores and numbers usually provide little information about the program context or the triggering fault.

Sometimes, words are combined using the camel case naming convention [98] instead of underscores. Therefore, DECAF further breaks down the consecutive letters based on the camel case rule. Specifically, DECAF separates the letters before each upper case letter if that letter is preceeded by a lower case letter. For instance, consecutive letters "helloWorld" will be separated into words "hello" and "World".

Finally, to handle acronyms in the identifiers, DECAF divides the consecutive letters before each upper case letter that is followed by a lower case letter. For example, consecutive letters "SSHConnection" will be divided into words "SSH" and "Connection".

### 4.3.4 DECAF Evaluation

**Methodology**

The evaluation of DECAF aims to answer the following research questions: (i) How effective is DECAF in detecting inaccurate exceptions? (ii) How does DECAF compare with DIET, a supervised approach for detecting inaccurate exceptions?

Table 4.3: The Evaluated Pruning Strengths.

| Pruning Strength | $N_{convention}$ | $N_{freq}$ |
|---|---|---|
| **No Pruning** | $\infty$ | 0 |
| **Moderate Pruning** | 10 | 5 |
| **Extreme Pruning** | 5 | 10 |

To facilitate a fair comparison with DIET, we apply DECAF to the same systems that we used to evaluate DIET. These systems are Cassandra-3.11.5, Hadoop-3.1.2, HBase-2.1.4, and ZooKeeper-2.4.14.

To answer the first research question, we calculate the number of inaccurate exceptions that DECAF detects in the target systems. Recall that DECAF's pruning step have two configurable thresholds, i.e., $N_{convention}$ and $N_{freq}$. To understand how different pruning strengths affect DECAF's effectiveness, we compare the number of inaccurate exceptions detected by DECAF when the thresholds are configured with different values. Specifically, we evaluate three pairs of threshold values to test how no pruning, moderate pruning, and extreme pruning affect DECAF's effectiveness. Table 4.3 shows the threshold values for these three pruning strengths.

Since DECAF ranks the exception objects based on their accuracy scores (from lowest to highest). It is up to developers to decide how many top-ranked exceptions to consider. Therefore, we also evaluate DECAF's effectiveness under different test budgets. Specifically, we evaluate DECAF's effectiveness when considering the 10, 20, and 50 top-ranked exceptions.

To answer the second research question, we configure DECAF using the best performing pruning scenario (based on the evaluation results of the first research question), and apply

Table 4.4: The Effectiveness of DECAF under Different Configurations.

| System | Budget | Pruning Strength[†] | | |
|---|---|---|---|---|
| | | No Pruning | Moderate Pruning | Extreme Pruning |
| Cassandra | 10 | 10 / 4 / 60% | 10 / 4 / 60% | 8 / 4 / 50% |
| | 20 | 20 / 5 / 75% | 20 / 6 / 70% | 8 / 4 / 50% |
| | 50 | 50 / 11 / 78% | 50 / 16 / 68% | 8 / 4 /50% |
| Hadoop | 10 | 10 / 2 / 80% | 10 / 3 / 70% | 10 / 3 / 70% |
| | 20 | 20 / 4 / 80% | 20 / 5 / 75% | 20 / 7 / 65% |
| | 50 | 50 / 10 / 80% | 50 / 15 / 70% | 47 / 14 / 70% |
| HBase | 10 | 10 / 2 / 80% | 10 / 2 / 80% | 10 / 4 / 60% |
| | 20 | 20 / 4 / 80% | 20 / 5 / 75% | 16 / 7 / 56% |
| | 50 | 50 / 14 / 72% | 50 / 18 / 64% | 16 / 7 / 56% |

[†]The numbers in each cell shows the number of inaccurate exceptions reported by DECAF, the number of reported exceptions that are indeed inaccurate, and the false positive rate of the corresponding configuration.

DECAF to the target systems. Moreover, for each target system, we give DECAF a test budget of $N$ inaccurate exceptions, where $N$ is the number of inaccurate exceptions reported by DIET for that target system (§4.2.4). Then we compare the number of inaccurate exceptions detected by DECAF and DIET.

**Evaluation Result**

Table 4.4 shows the effectiveness of DECAF when being configured with different pruning strengths and different test budgets. Specifically, the table lists the number of inaccurate exceptions reported by DECAF, the number of the reported exceptions that are indeed inaccurate, and the false positive rate under different configurations. The data for ZooKeeper is not listed in the table because DECAF reports only 3 and 0 inaccurate exceptions under the moderate pruning and the extreme pruning configurations.

```
class ViewDefinition {
  List<Relation> whereClauseToRelations(...) {
    try {
      CQLFregmentParser.parseAnyUnhandled(...);
    } catch (SyntaxException e) {
      // Inaccurate.
      throw new RuntimeException("Error parsing ...", e);
    }
  }
}

class CassandraServer {
  CqlResult execute_cql3_query(...) {
    try {
      // Indirectly calls whereClauseToRelations()
      return cqlQueryHandler.process(...);
    } catch (InvalidRequestException e) {
      informClient(e);
    }
  }
}
```

Figure 4.13: An Inaccurate Exception Detected by DECAF.

As shown by Table 4.4, DECAF is effective in detecting inaccurate exceptions. Specifically, DECAF detects inaccurate exceptions in all three target system under every configuration. Moreover, DECAF also detects one inaccurate exception in ZooKeeper under the moderate pruning strength in every test budget (not shown in the table).

Figure 4.13 shows an inaccurate exception detected by DECAF. When a Cassandra server parses an invalid user request, method `parseAnyUnhandled()` will throw a `SyntaxException` (Line 4). Method `whereClauseToRelations()` catches this exception and incorrectly rethrows a `RuntimeException` to signal the caller about the fault

(Lines 5–8). The exception class RuntimeException is inaccurate because it does not indicate that the user request is invalid. As a result, even though the caller method tries to catch InvalidRequestException (a superclass of SyntaxException) and inform the user about the fault (Lines 17–19), the exception handler will not be executed because the RuntimeException will not be caught by the catch statement (Line 17). Moreover, the thread handling the request will be crashed by the unhandled RuntimeException. DE-CAF detects this inaccurate exception because the exception class, RuntimeException, is inconsistent with the program context. Specifically, when handling a SyntaxException, Cassandra developers usually rethrow an InvalidRequestException to accurately represent the syntax error in the user request.

Table 4.4 also shows that, as the pruning strength increases, the false positive rate drops. For example, when analyzing Hadoop with a test budget of 20 inaccurate exceptions, the false positive rate for no pruning, moderate pruning, and extreme pruning strengths are 80%, 75%, and 65%, respectively. However, extreme pruning can remove a substantial amount of inaccurate exceptions from the reported candidates. For example, when analyzing Cassandra and HBase with a test budget of 50 inaccurate exceptions, the extreme pruning strength detects much less inaccurate exceptions when comparing to the moderate pruning (4 vs. 16 in Cassandra and 7 vs. 18 in HBase).

Figure 4.14 shows an inaccurate exceptions that is detected under the moderate pruning strength but not the extreme pruning. When an HBase replication thread is interrupted, method interruptOrAbortWhenFail() will throw a RuntimeException (Line 3). This exception is inaccurate because the RuntimeException class does not indicate that the thread is interrupted. Due to the inaccurate exception class, the dedicated catch block does not catch the exception (Lines 12–14), and the replication thread crashes without

```
1  class ReplicationSourceManager {
2    void interruptOrAbortWhenFail(...) {
3      throw new RuntimeException("Thread is interrupted.");
4    }
5  }
6
7  class ReplicationSourceShipper {
8    void run() {
9      try {
10       // Indirectly calls interruptOrAbortWhenFail()
11       shipEdits(...);
12     } catch (InterruptedException e) {
13       Thread.currentThread().interrupt();
14     }
15     cleanup();
16   }
17 }
```

Figure 4.14: An Inaccurate Exception that Is Pruned by Extreme Pruning.

Table 4.5: Comparion between DECAF and DIET.

| System | Tool | Reported Inaccurate Exceptions | | | |
| --- | --- | --- | --- | --- | --- |
| | | Total | Bug | Bad Practice | False Positive[†] |
| Cassandra | DECAF | 59 | 2 | 17 | 40 (67.8%) |
| | DIET | 100 | 0 | 9 | 91 (91%) |
| Hadoop | DECAF | 136 | 6 | 31 | 99 (72.79%) |
| | DIET | 136 | 2 | 18 | 116 (85.29%) |
| HBase | DECAF | 60 | 2 | 18 | 40 (66.67%) |
| | DIET | 73 | 0 | 2 | 71 (97.26%) |
| ZooKeeper | DECAF | 3 | 0 | 1 | 2 (66.67%) |
| | DIET | 5 | 0 | 0 | 5 (100%) |

[†]Column "False Positive" shows both the number of false positives and the corresponding false positive rate.

proper clean up (Line 15). As a result, the HBase server is left in an inconsistent state. DECAF detects this inaccurate exception because the exception class, `RuntimeException`, is inconsistent with the error message. In HBase, this error message is most consistent with class `InterruptedIOException`. Specifically, this error message co-appears with `InterruptedIOException` 8 times as frequently as `RuntimeException`. However, since the extreme pruning requires 10 times frequency to consider the message as frequently co-appearing with an exception class, this inaccurate exception is pruned by the extreme pruning. Based on Table 4.4, DECAF performs best under moderate pruning.

Table 4.5 shows the comparison between DECAF and DIET. Specifically, the table lists the number of inaccurate exceptions reported by each tool, and the corresponding bugs, bad practices, and false positives. In this experiment, DECAF is configured with moderate pruning. Even though we grant DECAF with a test budget that is the same as the number of

```
1  class StorageService {
2    void decommission() {
3      try {
4        ...
5      } catch (InterruptedException e) {
6        throw new RuntimeException("Node␣interrupted");
7      }
8    }
9  }
```

Figure 4.15: CASSANDRA-15113, a Bad Practice Detected by DIET.

inaccurate exceptions reported by DIET, DECAF may report less inaccurate exceptions due to the pruning effect. As the table shows, with the same budget, DECAF detects more bugs and more bad practices in all four systems. Therefore, DECAF also achieves lower false positive rates.

To further understand why DECAF detects more true inaccurate exceptions than DIET, we calculate the number of true inaccurate exceptions that do not have an error message, which cannot be analyzed by DIET. We find that only 4 out of the 77 true inaccurate exceptions do not have an error message. Therefore, DECAF's effectiveness in detecting inaccurate exceptions mainly come from its novel approach for identifying inconsistent feature values.

It is worth noting that, even though DECAF detects more inaccurate exceptions than DIET, only 4 bad practices are detected by both tools. As a result, DECAF and DIET are largely complimentary. For example, Figure 4.15 shows the root cause of CASSANDRA-15113, a bad practice detected by DIET but not DECAF. DIET detects this bad practice because the RuntimeException class implies a semantic condition while the error message implies an untimely interrupt. However, DECAF does not detect this bad practice because most of the interrupt-related error messages in Cassandra co-appear with class `RuntimeException`.

## 4.4  Summary

Inaccurate exceptions widely exist in cloud systems and can cause serious cloud system failures. This chapter presents DIET and DECAF, two techniques for detecting inaccurate exceptions. Experiments with four popular cloud systems show that both DIET and DECAF are effective in detecting inaccurate exceptions and are complimentary with each other.

**Chapter 5: Exposing FTBugs in Cloud Systems**

Chapter 4 presents two approaches to detect fault tolerance bugs, i.e., FTBugs, by analyzing the source code of the cloud system. Unfortunately, not all FTBugs can be detected using static approaches due to the absence of runtime information. Another way to uncover FTBugs is to expose them through executing the program. However, exposing FTBugs is challenging since the triggering process of an FTBug often requires the fault to occur in certain system states. In this chapter, we propose CoFI, a fault injection technique that automatically identifies vulnerable system states and injects faults to expose FTBugs.

## 5.1 Overview

Cloud systems run on networked commodity machines, where network partitions can occur as frequently as once a week and one incident may last for minutes or even hours [2]. Therefore, dependable cloud systems must handle network partitions correctly. Unfortunately, this is a challenging task since network partitions can happen to any node and can *start* and *stop at any time*. Even though developers strive to handle network partitions throughout designing, implementing, and testing a cloud system, network partitions can still lead to cloud system failures [2, 21].

Figure 5.1 uses a three-node replica-based cloud system to illustrate the typical process when a cloud system encounters a network partition. Normally, different nodes in a cloud

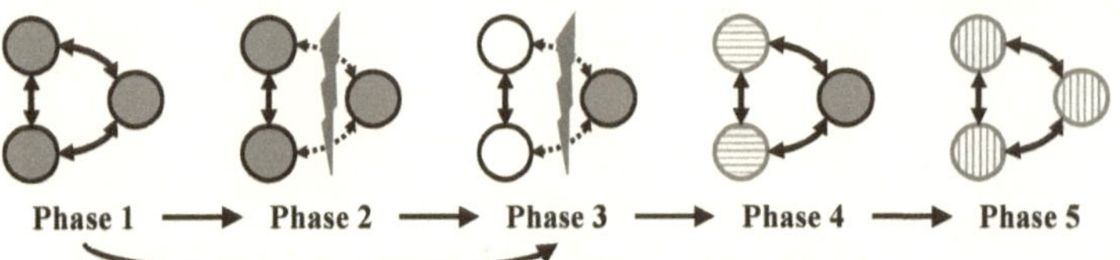


Each circle represents one node. Circles with the same pattern (i.e., solid, hollow, horizonal stripe, or vertical stripe) represent nodes that are consistent. In Phase 2 and 3, the lightnings represent network partitions, and the dotted arrows represent the message attempts failed by the network partition.

Figure 5.1: A Network Partition's Effect on a Three-Node Cluster.

system keep their states consistent by exchanging messages (Phase 1). When a network partition starts, the nodes on the different sides of the partition become disconnected. This may occur when the three nodes have consistent states (Phase 2). However, the two nodes on the left side may change their states later (e.g., serving a data update request from the client), causing inconsistency between the two sides (Phase 2 to Phase 3). Similarly, a network partition may occur when the two nodes on the left are already inconsistent with the node on the right (Phase 1 to Phase 3). This is possible because in cloud systems node states are updated asynchronously. When a network partition starts, cloud systems often have various built-in mechanisms to recover from inconsistent states, e.g., repeatedly trying to connect the partitioned nodes for recovery. Thus, cloud systems can still operate without the partitioned nodes. When the network heals, the two sides of the partition may have inconsistent states (Phase 4). In this case, the cloud system will try to recover the whole cluster back to a consistent state (Phase 5). We refer to the FTBugs triggered by network partitions as *partition bugs*. A partition bug can occur if the cloud system cannot tolerate the network disconnection in Phases 2 or 3, or cannot tolerate the inconsistency caused by the network partition in Phases 3 or 4.

Fault injection is a popular technique for testing cloud systems against faults, e.g., node crashes and network partitions. Many works inject node crashes when testing cloud systems [1,75,77]. However, node crashes and network partitions are fundamentally different. First, node crashes and network partitions often exercise different fault tolerance routines of a cloud system. Second, crashing a node will remove its in-memory state, while partitioning a node will not. So, these node-crashing injection techniques are inapplicable to expose partition bugs in cloud systems. Recently, a few tools have been proposed to inject network faults when testing cloud systems. For example, Namazu randomly drops network packages with a configured probability [86]. However, such a fault model resembles an unreliable network, which is different from network partitions. NEAT [2] and Jepsen [66] inject network partitions when testing cloud systems, but they rely on developers to specify when a network partition starts and stops.

To address this problem, this chapter proposes <u>Co</u>nsistency-guided <u>F</u>ault <u>I</u>njection (*CoFI*), an automated technique to expose partition bugs by systematically injecting network partitions into cloud systems. We find that *partition bugs are more likely to occur when cloud systems are running in inconsistent states* (i.e., Phases 3 and 4 in Figure 5.1) due to two main reasons. First, node communications at inconsistent states are harder to reason about than those at consistent states. Second, cloud systems strive to recover system states from inconsistency as quickly as possible, leaving smaller time windows for developers to test cloud systems at inconsistent states. Based on this observation, CoFI's main idea is to inject network partitions to thoroughly exercise cloud systems at inconsistent states.

Specifically, CoFI first employs distributed program invariants [34, 57] to represent the consistent states in a cloud system. A distributed program invariant (or invariant for short) is a property that must hold when multiple nodes are each at certain program point. Using invariants to represent consistent states allows CoFI to automatically identify consistent states in different cloud systems. Then, CoFI monitors the cloud system's runtime states and starts a network partition when an inconsistent state occurs, i.e., an invariant is temporarily violated. Starting the network partition in inconsistent states can prevent the cloud system from recovering back to consistency, so that CoFI can thoroughly test the cloud system at inconsistent states. Finally, CoFI systematically explores the stopping point of the network partition based on message types. Hence, CoFI enables more efficient testing of the cloud system than exhaustively stopping the partition for every message.

We have implemented a prototype of CoFI and applied it to multiple versions of three popular cloud systems, namely Cassandra [39], HDFS [48], and YARN [45]. CoFI can successfully detect 4 known bugs, and 12 *unknown* bugs that have never been reported before. Moreover, the triggering processes of 10 out of these 16 bugs have timing requirements on both the starting and the stopping points of the network partitions. At the time of this writing, developers have confirmed four of the 12 unknown bugs reported by CoFI. The CoFI prototype is publicly available at [23].

The rest of this chapter is organized as follows. §5.2 further motivates CoFI by dissecting a partition bug that can only be triggered if the network partition starts and stops at specific timing. §5.3 explains CoFI's design at length. §5.4 describes CoFI's implementation details. §5.5 discusses CoFI's evaluation. Finally, §5.6 summarizes this chapter.

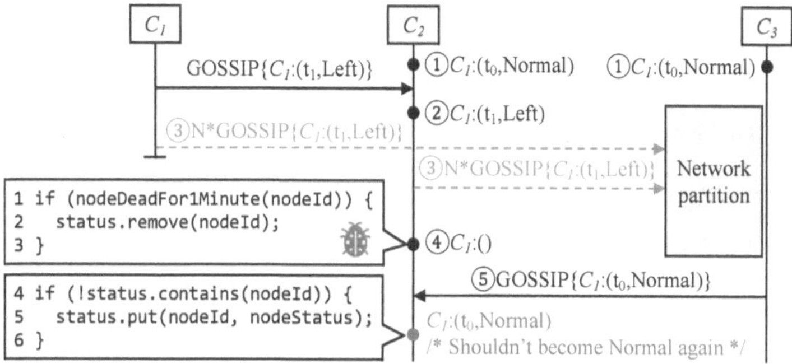



Figure 5.2: The Triggering Process of CASSANDRA-2115.

## 5.2 Motivation and Challenges

In this section, we first motivate consistency-guided fault injection (i.e., CoFI) with a real-world example. Then, we use the motivating example to discuss how CoFI addresses its main challenges.

### 5.2.1 A Motivating Example

**The Triggering Process**

Figure 5.2 shows the triggering process of CASSANDRA-2115, a partition bug that manifests when two Cassandra nodes exchange gossip messages at a specific inconsistent state. In a Cassandra cluster, each node obtains the status of its peers through exchanging gossip messages. Updates to a node's status are ordered using vector clocks. If $C_1$, $C_2$ and $C_3$ are the three nodes in a cluster, both $C_2$ and $C_3$ will know that $C_1$ is running normally (Step ①). The cluster is now in a consistent state (Phase 1 in Figure 5.1). When a user decommissions $C_1$, $C_1$ will change its status to "Left", increases its clock value (from $t_0$ to $t_1$), and then notifies its peers about the update. When $C_2$ receives the update message, it will modify its local copy accordingly (Step ②) since the incoming message has a greater clock value ($t_1 > t_0$). However, due to a network partition, $C_3$ does not receive any message about the update (Step ③). As a result, $C_3$ will falsely believe that $C_1$ is still running normally. At this moment, the cluster becomes partitioned and inconsistent (Phase 3 in Figure 5.1). After certain amount of time, $C_2$ drops $C_1$'s status, together with the clock value (Step ④). At this point, the network partition heals, allowing $C_2$ and $C_3$ to exchange messages at the inconsistent state where $C_2$ forgets about $C_1$ while $C_3$ thinks $C_1$ is running normally (Phase 4 in Figure 5.1). We use $\{\varnothing, \text{Normal}\}$ to denote this inconsistent state. $C_3$ then propagates to $C_2$ an outdated value of $C_1$'s status (Step ⑤). Since $C_2$ now knows nothing about $C_1$, it will blindly accept $C_3$'s value, even though it is outdated ($t_0 < t_1$). As a result, $C_1$ reappears to be running normally after it has already been decommissioned!

**Timing Requirements on Network Partitions**

To trigger this bug, $C_2$ and $C_3$ need to exchange a gossip message in the inconsistent state $\{\varnothing, \text{Normal}\}$. This requires the network partition to start after Step ① and before Step ③, as well as to stop after Step ④ and before Step ⑤. First, if the network partition starts before Step ①, $C_3$ will not consider $C_1$ as running normally. Second, if the network partition starts after Step ③ or stops before Step ④, $C_2$ and $C_3$ will eventually agree that $C_1$ has left. Finally, if the network partition does not stop before Step ⑤, $C_2$ and $C_3$ will not exchange gossip messages at state $\{\varnothing, \text{Normal}\}$. The bug will not be triggered if any of the aforementioned situations happens. Such a complex timing requirement on the network partition makes the bug difficult to be exposed using random or developer-specified fault injection.

## 5.2.2 Challenges and Solutions

To trigger the partition bug in our motivating example, CoFI injects network partitions to thoroughly test the cloud system in inconsistent states. CoFI needs to address the following three challenges.

**Challenge 1: How to Represent and Decide Consistent States?**

The consistency of a system state is closely related to the specific protocols that individual cloud system adopts. For example, Cassandra uses Paxos to replicate user data [40] while HDFS uses replication pipeline [48]. Moreover, even for the same protocol, two cloud systems may have their own implementations such as Cassandra's and Google Spanner's Paxos implementations [56]. CoFI employs *distributed program invariants* [34, 57] to represent the consistent states in a cloud system. A distributed program invariant is a property that must hold when multiple nodes are each at certain program point. For a selected invariant, a cloud system state is consistent if it satisfies the invariant. Otherwise, the state is inconsistent. We can use the following invariant to represent the consistent states in our motivating example, i.e., $C_2$ and $C_3$ agree on $C_1$'s status:

$$status[C_1]@C_2 == status[C_1]@C_3$$

From Figure 5.2 we can see that, at a consistent state, e.g., Step ①, the above invariant is satisfied. Conversely, at an inconsistent state, e.g., Step ②, the above invariant is violated. Since the invariants can be automatically extracted from cloud systems, such consistent states can be easily applied to different protocols and implementations.

**Challenge 2: When to Start a Network Partition?**

An intuitive idea is to start a network partition at every point during the system execution since it simulates the real-world scenario that the network can be partitioned at any time. However, this approach is impractical due to extremely high overhead. In our motivating example, Step ③ alone lasts for more than one minute, containing too many execution points to explore. Instead, CoFI injects a network partition as soon as it detects an inconsistent state at run time. For example, using the invariant in §5.2.2 to represent consistent states, CoFI will start the network partition after $C_2$ updates its local copy of $C_1$'s status to "Left" (Step ②) and before $C_3$ updates its local copy of $C_1$'s status to "Left". To provide maximum chances of exposing partition bugs, CoFI injects network partitions at the message level (instead of at the user operation level as employed by other tools [2, 66]) by failing the message exchanges among nodes. Therefore, the gossip messages at Step ③ will be failed, keeping $C_2$ and $C_3$ inconsistent.

**Challenge 3: When to Stop a Network Partition?**

To exercise a cloud system at inconsistent states, one can try to stop the network partition at every execution point (i.e., enabling message exchange before each message is sent). However, this approach of exhaustively searching all possible points to stop the network partition has very high overhead. For instance, Step ③ alone consists of more than 100 gossip messages. Trying to stop the network partition before each of them will be inefficient for exposing our motivating bug. To address this issue, CoFI classifies messages into different types and systematically explores the timing of stopping a network partition for each type of messages, instead of each message. After the classification, the gossip messages at Step ③ are grouped into only a few types, drastically reducing the number of stopping points to explore.

## 5.3 Consistency-Guided Fault Injection

In this section, we first discuss CoFI's fault model. Then, we explain CoFI's workflow and the major steps.

### 5.3.1 Fault Model

CoFI tests a cloud system by injecting a period of *temporary* network partition to *one* node in the system. Here, "temporary" means that a started network partition will stop at certain point. Note that starting a network partition at inconsistent states only tests the cloud system at Phase 3 in Figure 5.1. To thoroughly test a cloud system at inconsistent states, CoFI also stops the network partition to test the cloud system at Phase 4, i.e., exchanging messages among inconsistent nodes.

The specifics of our fault model are as follows. First, in a test run, only one node will be partitioned. Second, the network partition can start and stop at any time (controlled by CoFI), but CoFI will only start and stop the network partition once per test run. Third, during the network partition, all the messages being sent from or delivered to the partitioned node will be failed. CoFI focuses on this simple network partition model because it is realistic, and more importantly, cloud systems are expected to correctly handle such a simple fault model at the minimum. It is worth noting that CoFI can be extended to test more complicated fault models, e.g., partitioning multiple nodes and simplex partition [2].

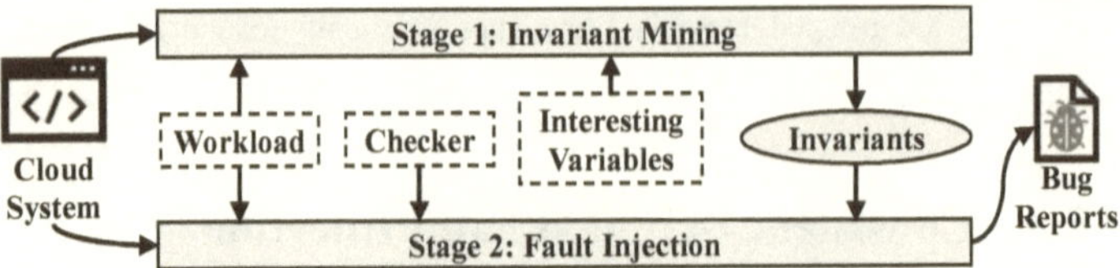



The two solid boxes represent the two stages of CoFI's workflow. The three dotted boxes represent the configurable inputs to each stage.

Figure 5.3: CoFI's Workflow.

### 5.3.2  CoFI in A Nutshell

Figure 5.3 presents an overview of CoFI's workflow. CoFI works in two stages: *invariant mining* and *fault injection*. In the invariant mining stage, CoFI first runs the cloud system using the workload and records the runtime values of the interesting variables. Then, CoFI mines distributed program invariants from the recorded variable values. The mined invariants will be used to guide starting and stopping network partitions in the fault injection stage. Specifically, for each invariant, which represents consistent system states, CoFI systematically explores the scenarios of network partitions that start at an inconsistent state where the invariant is violated and stop at a later execution point. During each testing run, CoFI uses the checker to detect incorrect system behaviors, e.g., system down. When the checker fails, CoFI will generate a detailed bug report to help developers diagnose the failure. The bug report contains information about the executed workload, the failure symptom, the runtime values of the invariant-related variables, as well as the messages failed by the network partition.

```
1  // NameNode's status on NameNode.
2  NameNode.instance.state: NameNode_Status
3  // NameNode's status on DataNode.
4  DataNode.instance.bpManager.bpByNameserviceId.bpServices.
     state: NameNode_Status
```

Figure 5.4: Two Interesting Variables in HDFS.


### 5.3.3  Specifying Interesting Variables

**Which Variables are Interesting?**

In the invariant mining stage, CoFI mines distributed program invariants based on the runtime values of some interesting variables. Which variables are interesting? We observe that two categories of variables can better represent the state of a cloud system, namely *system metadata* (e.g., the status of a Cassandra node as shown in our motivating example) and *user metadata* (e.g., the location of a container in YARN). This meta-information is critical because anything wrong with this meta-information may seriously affect the reliability of a cloud system. Moreover, an interesting variable should *have data flow from or to the network* so that CoFI can exercise the cloud system in inconsistent states by controlling the timing of the network partition. For instance, the $status[C1]$ variable in our motivating example is a system metadata that has data flow to and from the network. By starting the network partition when $C_2$ and $C_3$ are inconsistent on $status[C_1]$ (Step ③ in Figure 5.2) and stopping the network partition after $C_2$ removes its $status[C_1]$ (Step ④), CoFI triggers the bug.

**How to Specify Interesting Variables?**

Since CoFI may access an interesting variable outside of its scope, we represent an interesting variable using the path to access the variable from a Java `static` field (Java's global variable). We refer to these paths as *access paths*. Figure 5.4 lists two interesting variables (i.e., two access paths) that *refer to the same metadata* in HDFS. Specifically, these two variables both store the status of a NameNode, i.e., whether the NameNode is active or standby. When specifying an interesting variable, one should specify the access path followed by the metadata stored in the variable. Let's use the first interesting variable (Line 2) to further explain how the access path works. `NameNode.instance` is a `static` field that refers to a NameNode object, and `state` is the NameNode object's instance field that stores the NameNode's status. At run time, CoFI accesses this interesting variable by first accessing the `NameNode.instance` object and then accessing the `state` field of that `NameNode.instance` object. Developers can provide their own interesting variables to represent system states, customizing CoFI to test the states they are interested in. The effort needed to specify an interesting variable depends on the implementation details involved in the access path. For example, it is straightforward to derive the first access path in Figure 5.4 because it matches with "the NameNode's status". Conversely, specifying the second access path requires the knowledge that a DataNode stores information about the NameNodes in the `bpManager` field. The metadata after each access path is a user-defined identifier, which will help CoFI select interesting invariants in the invariant mining stage.

## 5.3.4 Invariant Mining

In the invariant mining stage, CoFI first runs the cloud system and records the interesting variables' values at the program points that likely reflect consistent system states. Then,

CoFI groups the values recorded on different nodes to reconstruct the consistent states, from which invariants are mined. Finally, from the mined invariants, CoFI selects the interesting ones to guide fault injection in the next stage.

**Which Program Points to Collect Variable Values?**

To derive consistent states in a cloud system, CoFI mines distributed program invariants from the interesting variables' runtime values at certain program points. The convention is to choose program points like function entrances, function exits, and loop entrances [34]. However, values at these program points may reflect the intermediate results of a node's local computation, which do not represent the system's consistent states. Instead, CoFI selects program points right before a message is sent (*before-send program points*) and right after a message is handled (*after-handle program points*). Specifically, CoFI considers the entrance of a message-sending method as a before-send program point, and considers the exit of a message-handling method as an after-handle program point. A before-send program point reflects the sender node's state when it has applied some changes locally, and is ready to propagate such a change to its peers. Similarly, an after-handle program point reflects the receiver node's state when it has finished updating its local state according to a received message. Therefore, the sender and the receiver of the same message are usually consistent at the pair of these program points.

Figure 5.5 illustrates such a property using our motivating example. It shows a partial execution of $C_2$ and $C_3$ if the network partition does not occur and $C_2$ sends a gossip message to $C_3$ at Step ③ in Figure 5.2. At the before-send program point (Line 3 in Figure 5.5), $C_2$ has updated its copy of $C_1$'s status (Line 2). At the after-handle program point (Line 8), $C_3$ has also updated its copy of $C_1$'s status according to the gossip message from $C_2$ (Line 7). As a result, $C_2$ and $C_3$ are consistent about $C_1$'s status at this pair of program points.

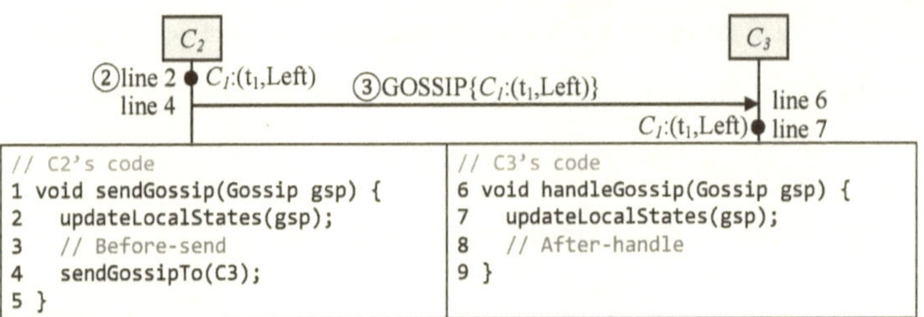


Figure 5.5: A Partial Execution of $C_2$ and $C_3$ if the Network Partition in Figure 5.2 Does Not Occur.

**How to Associate Values from Different Nodes?**

After collecting variable values at the before-send program points and the after-handle program points, CoFI needs to group these values to reconstruct the consistent states. Since the sender and the receiver of a message are usually consistent at the corresponding before-send and after-handle program points, CoFI groups the variable values at the pair of these program points to reconstruct the consistent state. For the example in Figure 5.5, CoFI groups $C_2$'s variable values at Line 3 and $C_3$'s variable values at Line 8 for the same gossip message to reconstruct the state. The constructed state contains all the variables logged at the two before-send and after-handle program point instances. CoFI considers the state of two nodes, i.e., pair-wise state, instead of the state of all the nodes in the cluster for two reasons. First, many properties of distributed protocols can be captured in pair-wise states. For instance, for Cassandra's gossip protocol, two nodes should be consistent after they have exchanged gossips (e.g., the invariant in §5.2.2). Second, even when a property involves more than two nodes, breaking the sub-property between any pair of the involved nodes will be sufficient to violate the whole property. For example, in HDFS's replication protocol, all the replicas should have the same data when a write succeeds. If any pair of replicas have different data, the whole property no longer holds. When the interesting variable is $status[C_1]$ in Figure 5.5, grouping $C_2$'s value at Line 3 and $C_3$'s value at Line 8 allows CoFI to mine the desired invariant, i.e., the invariant in §5.2.2.

**Which Invariants are More Interesting?**

After constructing the pair-wise states, CoFI employs Daikon [34] to perform the actual invariant mining. By default, Daikon can mine many invariants [57]. Exploring all these invariants can be very time-consuming. Therefore, CoFI further prunes the mined invariants based on a few heuristics, allowing developers to run more interesting tests within a limited budget.

First, CoFI only selects invariants that involve multiple (i.e., two in our setting) nodes. Cross-node invariants capture the consistent states of different nodes. When they are violated, the involved nodes are inconsistent. Second, CoFI removes invariants among variables that refer to different metadata because it may not be meaningful to compare two different metadata. Record that, when specifying an interesting variable, developers also specify the metadata referred to by the variable (§5.3.3). If an invariant involves variables that refer to different metadata, the invariant will be disregarded. By default, Daikon mines many types of invariants, e.g., the equality of variable values (e.g., $var_a == var_b + var_c$), and the membership relation between two variables (e.g., $var_{elmnt} \in var_{set}$). CoFI focuses on equality invariants since it is usually easier to violate these invariants, i.e., to create inconsistent states, during the test runs. Since the invariant for triggering CASSANDRA-2115 asserts the equality of the same metadata on two nodes, CoFI will select it.

Note that, CoFI's methodology allows using any invariant to represent consistent states, pruning out less interesting invariants improves the test efficiency.

---

**Algorithm 1:** Running Fault Injection Tests for An Invariant.

---

**Input:** invariant, workload, checker

1   iStates := runWithoutPartition(invariant)

2   **while** *iState := iStates.next()* **do**

3     **for** *iNd $\in$ iState.inconsistentNodes* **do**

4       passedNewMsgType := true; allMsgTypes := { }

5       **while** *passedNewMsgType* **do**

6         (newIStates, passedNewMsgType) := runWithPartition(iState, allMsgTypes)

7         iStates.add(newIStates)

8   **Function** *runWithPartition(iState, allMsgTps)* **do**

9     workload.start()

10    partition := WAITING; passedNewMsgTp := false

11    **while** *workload.isRunning* **do**

12      **if** *partition = WAITING $\wedge$ curState = iState* **then**

13       partition := STARTED

14      **if** *partition = STARTED $\wedge$ curMsg $\notin$ allMsgTps* **then**

15       allMsgTps.add(curMsg)

16       passedNewMsgTp := true; partition := STOPPED

17    **if** *checker.failed* **then**

18      generateBugReport()

19    **return** (getNewInconsistentStates(), passedNewMsgTp)

---

### 5.3.5   Fault Injection

In the fault injection stage, CoFI conducts multiple test runs for each mined invariant, as shown in Algorithm 1. More specifically, for each invariant, CoFI first runs the cloud system without injecting network partition to record possible inconsistent states for starting the network partition in the later runs (Line 1). Then, CoFI iterates over each inconsistent state as the starting point of a network partition (Line 2). For each inconsistent state, CoFI also explores partitioning different inconsistent nodes (Line 3). For each <inconsistent state,

partitioned node> pair, CoFI repeatedly runs the cloud system to systematically explore different scenarios of network partitions described as follows.

In each test run for exploring one scenario of a network partition, CoFI first starts the workload (Line 9) and monitors the cloud system's runtime state (represented by the invariant-related variables). Once the system reaches the selected inconsistent state of the current run, CoFI starts the network partition by stopping future messages sending from or delivering to the partitioned node (Lines 12-13). CoFI systematically explores different network partition stopping points by stopping the network partition before different types of messages.

For each message type, CoFI explores two possible cases: stopping the network partition or maintaining the network partition at this point. Specifically, after the network partition starts, CoFI intercepts every message that is sending from or delivering to the partitioned node. If having not seen the type of an intercepted message, CoFI explores the scenario of stopping the partition at this point, which allows the current and future messages to pass (Lines 14-16). Otherwise, CoFI maintains the network partition by dropping the message. CoFI simulates message drop at the application level instead of the OS level. More details will be explained in §5.4. At the end of each test run, if the checker fails, CoFI generates a bug report for the failure (Lines 17-18). CoFI terminates exploring the scenarios of the network partition for the pair of <inconsistent state, partitioned node> if there is no new message type encountered in the latest run (Line 5), which means CoFI has explored both passing and failing all the message types.

Due to the non-determinism in the cloud system's execution, some inconsistent states may not occur in the first partition-free run but in the later runs. Therefore, CoFI continues collecting new inconsistent states in each test run (Line 19). The newly collected inconsistent

states will be used as the starting point of the network partition in the successive runs (Line 7).
It is also possible that some inconsistent states CoFI initially collected may not occur in
the later test runs. To address this issue, CoFI will retry the test runs multiple times (a
configurable parameter) for the inconsistent state.

**Identifying Inconsistent States**

To identify the possible inconsistent states during the partition-free run (Line 1 in Algorithm 1) and the runs with network partitions (Line 6 in Algorithm 1), CoFI monitors the
runtime values of the interesting variables. Specifically, CoFI synchronously collects the
variable values at the before-send program points and the after-handle program points. By
collecting values at the after-handle program points, CoFI can capture the state change that is
caused by a node handling a state-changing message. As shown in our motivating example,
after $C_2$ handles $C_1$'s gossip message at Step ② in Figure 5.2, CoFI will immediately know
that $status[C_1]@C_2$ has become "Left". Sometimes, a state change is not caused by the node
handling a message. For example, Step ④ in Figure 5.2 happens after a timeout (Line 1
in Figure 5.2). To capture these state changes, CoFI collects the variable values at the
before-send program points. Since cloud systems often employ a heartbeat mechanism,
collecting variable values at before-send program points helps CoFI periodically refresh its
copy of a node's state. When $C_2$ tries to send a gossip after Step ④ in Figure 5.2, CoFI will
realize that $status[C_1]@C_2$ has become $\varnothing$.

**Classifying Messages**

When CoFI fails a message during a network partition, the cloud system can react in
two ways: The cloud system can simply retry sending the message, or initiate a different
protocol to perform recovery (e.g., Cassandra will initiate hinted-handoff when a data

replication message fails). Stopping the network partition for retried messages is unnecessary since exchanging the same type of messages will not exercise the cloud system differently. However, stopping the network partition in the second scenario can test if the alternative protocol will proceed correctly at inconsistent states.

Based on this observation, CoFI systematically explores stopping the network partition before each *type* of messages (Lines 14-16 in Algorithm 1), instead of each message. An ideal message type should correlate with the code segments that will be executed when sending or handling the message. In this way, stopping the network partition before different types of messages may exercise different code segments in the cloud system.

CoFI represents the message type using the quad `<stack, sender, receiver, state>`, where `stack` is the runtime call stack of the message sending method, `sender` and `receiver` are the sender and the receiver of the message, and `state` is the system state (i.e., the values of the invariant-related variables) when the message is sent. The message type includes the sender call stack of a message because it reflects the execution path on the sender side. Moreover, messages sent at different call stacks usually belong to different protocols (e.g., Cassandra's gossip and hinted-handoff protocols), or different steps of the same protocol (e.g., the commit-request step and the commit step of a two-phase commit protocol [99]). Therefore, handling messages with different sender call stack will likely execute different code segments on the receiver side. The other three elements in the message type also correlate with the code segments that will be exercised. In our motivating example, the following three types of messages execute different code segments at the receiver side:

$$\text{Type 1: } <\text{stack}_{\text{gossip}}, C_2, C_3, \{\text{Left, Normal}\}>$$
$$\text{Type 2: } <\text{stack}_{\text{gossip}}, C_3, C_2, \{\text{Left, Normal}\}>$$
$$\text{Type 3: } <\text{stack}_{\text{gossip}}, C_3, C_2, \{\varnothing, \text{Normal}\}>$$

Specifically, a Type 1 message will trigger the code that checks the message's vector clock and updates the receiver's state, a Type 2 message will exercise the code that checks the message's vector clock and discards the message, and a Type 3 message will execute the code that blindly accepts the value in the message. For example, all the gossip messages that $C_2$ sends to $C_3$ at Step ③ in Figure 5.2 belong to Type 1. As a result, CoFI will not redundantly try to stop the network partition before each of these equivalent gossip messages.

### 5.3.6  Workload and Checker

Workloads drive CoFI to exercise a target cloud system. They can come from various sources ranging from simple unit tests to carefully-crafted test cases for stress testing. Although CoFI can be driven by different workloads, CoFI is most effective when the workload includes cross-node operations that repeatedly read and write the interesting variables in different ways. With such a workload, CoFI can explore more network partition scenarios. For each of our tested cloud system, we implement a few such workloads using common admin operations (e.g., ResourceManager failover in YARN) and user operations (e.g., file movement in HDFS).

Moreover, developers can flexibly implement checkers to assert the system properties they care about. We provide default checkers in CoFI, one per workload. Specifically, our checkers check for both general failures (i.e., FATAL entries, ERROR entries, and exceptions in execution logs, as well as node crashes) and operation-specific failures (e.g., returning error code and reading stale data).

## 5.4   Implementation

CoFI has three components: an instrumentation engine, an invariant mining engine, and a fault injection engine. The instrumentation engine instruments the cloud system to enable reading the interesting variables at run time as well as intercepting message sending and message handling method calls. The invariant mining engine runs the cloud system and mines distributed program invariants from the values recorded by the instrumented code. The fault injection engine runs the workload and the checker on the cloud system and interacts with the instrumented code to inject network partitions.

### 5.4.1   Code Instrumentation

We build CoFI's instrumentation engine using Javassist [24], a Java bytecode instrumentation toolkit. To enable accessing interesting variables at run time, the instrumentation engine adds a getter method for each field in the target system. To intercept message sending method calls, the instrumentation engine adds a call to CoFI's `beforeSend()` API at the beginning of each message sending method (i.e., each before-send program point). Similarly, to intercept message handling method calls, the instrumentation engine adds a call to CoFI's `afterHandle()` API at the end of each message handling method (i.e., each after-handle program point). We integrate CoFI with the knowledge of the message sending methods and the message handling methods in popular cloud systems, e.g., `sendOneWay()` in Cassandra. Developers can configure CoFI to instrument different message-passing methods. Inside the message sending methods, the instrumentation engine also adds code to simulate the network partition's effect on the local node. In the fault injection stage, this code will be executed when the fault injection engine decides to fail the message. Developers can also configure the effect of the network partition. By default, the instrumented code throws an `IOException`.

Both `beforeSend()` and `afterHandle()` take three parameters: the sender of the message, the receiver of the message, and the class of the message. All three parameters are used to generate an ID for the message in the invariant mining stage. The sender and the receiver parameters are also sent to the fault injection engine to decide the message type during the fault injection stage.

## 5.4.2 Invariant Mining

In the invariant mining stage, `beforeSend()` and `afterHandle()` perform similar tasks: Both APIs first record the interesting variables' values through calling the getter methods. Then, the APIs generate an ID for the message-to-send or the handled message. Finally, they associate the variable values with the message ID and write them to a log, from which the invariant mining engine mines invariants.

Note that CoFI needs to pair the before-send and after-handle program points of the same message to reconstruct a system state. To identify the same message on the sender and receiver sides, CoFI makes two assumptions: (i) Each communication channel between two nodes is FIFO; (ii) Messages of the same class go through the same channel. Take our motivating bug as an example, under these two assumptions, the first gossip message that $C_2$ sends to $C_3$ is the first gossip message that $C_3$ receives from $C_2$. All of our tested systems satisfy these two assumptions. With these assumptions, CoFI constructs the message ID to be the concatenation of the message's sender, receiver, class, and the counter $i$. In this way, a message will have the same ID on the sender and receiver sides.

When mining invariants, the invariant mining engine first groups the variable values at the before-send program point and the after-handle program point of the same message to form a system state. The engine then concatenates the states of the same program point pair (i.e., same sender, same receiver, and same message class) to form a trace of the states for that program point pair. Afterwards, the engine runs Daikon [34] on the traces to mine invariants. Finally, the mined invariants are pruned based on the rules in §5.3.4.

### 5.4.3 Fault Injection

In the fault injection stage, the `beforeSend()` and the `afterHandle()` APIs record the runtime values of the invariant-related variables and report them to the fault injection engine. The `beforeSend()` API also reports the pending message sending event to the fault injection engine, and waits for the engine's decision on whether the message should be failed. If the engine decides to fail the message, the `beforeSend()` API will return a `false`, triggering the execution of the instrumented code in its caller (i.e., the message sending method) to simulate the network partition, e.g., by throwing an `IOException` to signal the caller about the network partition, or by returning from the message sending method to simulate a silent message drop.

## 5.5 Evaluation

Our evaluation aims to answer three research questions: (1) How effective is CoFI in detecting partition bugs in cloud systems? (2) How does CoFI compare with other approaches for injecting network partitions? (3) How efficient is CoFI? We perform our evaluation using a CloudLab [32] machine that runs Ubuntu 16.04. The machine has 40 Xeon® E5-2660 processors and 157 GB memory.

Table 5.1: The Known Bugs Used to Evaluate CoFI.

| Bug ID | Stop[†] | Operations[‡] | Interesting Metadata |
|---|---|---|---|
| CASSANDRA-3975 | ✓ | Write data, drop table | Column family name |
| CASSANDRA-2115 | ✓ | Decommission node | Node status |
| HDFS-14372 | × | Shutdown DataNode | DataNode ID |
| YARN-4288 | × | Start cluster | NodeManager ID |

[†]Column "Stop" shows whether the bug requires stopping a network partition to trigger. [‡]Column "Operations" shows the operations in the workload for exposing each bug.

### 5.5.1 Experimental Methodology

**Target Cloud Systems**

We select three widely-used open-source cloud systems as our experiment subjects, i.e., Cassandra [39], HDFS [48], and YARN [45]. They represent different kinds of cloud systems. First, they provide different functionalities: Cassandra is a distributed NoSQL database, HDFS is a distributed file system, and YARN is a distributed computing framework. Moreover, these systems adopt different system architectures: Cassandra is a peer-to-peer system while HDFS and YARN are coordinator/worker systems. Finally, to combat network partitions, these systems implement different recovery mechanisms, e.g., HDFS employs data re-replication to recover inconsistent user data [48], and Cassandra uses gossip to recover inconsistent system metadata [42].

**Detecting Partition Bugs**

To evaluate CoFI's effectiveness, we apply CoFI to our target systems and check if CoFI can detect both known bugs and unknown bugs.

First, we collect several known partition bugs by inspecting the recently published bug datasets [2, 21, 72, 77]. If a bug satisfies the following requirements, we select it to evaluate CoFI: (1) It happens in our target systems. (2) It only requires partitioning one node to trigger. (3) We can manually reproduce the bug. Finally, we obtained four partition bugs, as shown in Table 5.1. These four known bugs cover all three target systems, and have different timing requirements on the network partition (Column "Stop"). Table 5.1 also shows the operations in each bug's workload (Column "Operations") and the metadata stored in the interesting variables which we specify for each bug (Column "Interesting Metadata"). The operations are extracted from the bug reports. The interesting variables are identified through understanding each bug's triggering process.

To evaluate CoFI's effectiveness in detecting unknown bugs, we apply CoFI to test the latest versions (at the time of this writing) of our target systems. For HDFS and YARN, we test both their version 2 and version 3 since these versions are both widely deployed and under active development. For Cassandra, we only test its version 3 since the latest minor release of its version 2 (Cassandra-2.2) will no longer be supported after Cassandra's next major release [41]. Specifically, the target system versions are Cassandra-3.11.5, HDFS-3.3.0, HDFS-2.10.0, YARN-3.3.0, and YARN-2.10.0.

We design several workloads for each target system using the common user and admin operations as shown in Table 5.2. For HDFS and YARN, we use the same set of operations for both of their versions. The operations in each workload follow natural order, e.g., create a table before writing data to it. For Cassandra-3, we implement four workloads on a three-node cluster to test regular data access, Paxos data access, schema update, and node decommission. For both HDFS-2 and HDFS-3, we design three workloads to test file system operations, NameNode failover, and DataNode failover. Both the file system operations

Table 5.2: Operations in the Test Workloads.

| System | Operations in the Test Workloads |
| --- | --- |
| Cassandra | Create keyspace/column family, read/write data, add/remove column, decommission node |
| HDFS | Read/write file, move file/directory, failover NameNode, failover DataNode |
| YARN | Launch/stop application, failover NodeManager, failover ResourceManager |

workload and the NameNode failover workload run on a cluster of two NameNodes and three DataNodes while the DataNode failover workload runs on a cluster with two NameNodes and four DataNodes. For YARN-2, we create three workloads: Run a YARN application in a cluster of one ResourceManager and one NodeManager; ResourceManager failover in a cluster of two ResourceManagers and one NodeManager; NodeManager failover in a cluster of two ResourceManagers and two NodeManagers. For YARN-3, we build two workloads: ResourceManager failover when a YARN application is running in a cluster of two ResourceManagers and one NodeManager; NodeManager failover when a YARN application is running in a cluster of two ResourceManagers and two NodeManagers. Moreover, each YARN cluster also runs on top of an HDFS cluster with one NameNode and one DataNode.

Our checkers check for both general failures (i.e., FATAL entries, ERROR entries, and exceptions in execution logs, as well as node crashes) and operation-specific failures (e.g., returning an error code and reading stale data). To explore more network partition scenarios, we limit at most 100 fault injection runs for each invariant.

Table 5.3: The Interesting Metadata Selected for Each Target System.

| System | Interesting Metadata | Var #[†] |
|---|---|---|
| Cassandra-3.11.5 | Node Status, node token, keyspace name | 3 |
| HDFS-3.3.0 | DataNode ID, NameNode ID, NameNode status, data block ID, data block location | 9 |
| HDFS-2.10.0 | DataNode ID, NameNode ID, NameNode status, data block ID, data block location | 9 |
| YARN-3.3.0 | NodeManager ID, container ID, container location, ResourceManager ID, ResourceManager status | 9 |
| YARN-2.10.0 | NodeManager ID, container ID, container location, ResourceManager ID, ResourceManager status | 9 |

[†]Column "Var #" shows the number of interesting variables in each system.

Table 5.3 shows the metadata stored in the interesting variables that we specify for each target system. For Cassandra-3, we specify the interesting variable that stores keyspace name instead of column family name as for triggering `CASSANDRA-3975`. This is because keyspace names are accessed more often than column family names (to access a column family, one needs to first access the owner keyspace), potentially exposing more system behaviors when two nodes are inconsistent on a keyspace name. To enable accessing the interesting variables in HDFS and YARN, we add two `static` fields to each version of HDFS and three `static` fields to each version of YARN to refer to the objects of the main components in the system, i.e., NameNode, DataNode, ResourceManager, NodeManager, and ApplicationMaster. In total, this only involves modifying 22 lines of code for all four system versions. The manual efforts for specifying the interesting variables are acceptable: It only takes one person a few hours to specify all the interesting variables and implemented all the modifications in the target systems, even though that person only has a basic understanding of these systems. For the developers of these systems, specifying interesting variables should take much less time.

**Comparing with an Alternative Approach.**

We compare CoFI with injecting network partitions *randomly*. To be more specific, we repeatedly run each workload for the same time as CoFI spends when testing the target systems. During each test run, we inject a network partition randomly. The scenario of the network partition is determined before each test run. First, we randomly select a node to inject network partition. Then, we decide when to start and stop the network partition. The starting point and the stopping point of the network partition are represented using the time offset from the start of a test run. We randomly choose a time offset between 0 and the longest test duration to be the starting point of the network partition, and randomly select a time offset between the starting point and the longest test duration to be the stopping point of the network partition. The longest test duration will be updated when a longer test run occurs. If a test run finishes before the starting point/stopping point is reached, the network partition does not start/stop in that test run.

## 5.5.2   Detecting Partition Bugs

### Overall Experimental Results

Table 5.4 lists the partition bugs triggered by CoFI. In this table, we show the detailed information about each bug, including the bug's ID in JIRA (Column "Bug ID"), the failure symptom of the bug (Column "Failure Symptom"), the interesting metadata in the invariant that guides CoFI to expose the bug (Column "Interesting Metadata"), and whether the bug requires stopping the network partition to trigger (Column "Stop").

Table 5.4: Bugs Triggered by CoFI.

| Bug ID | Failure Symptom | Interesting Metadata | Stop[†] |
|---|---|---|---|
| Known Bugs | | | |
| CASSANDRA-3975 | Thread keeps crashing | Column family name | ✓ |
| CASSANDRA-2115 | Removed node reappears | Node status | ✓ |
| HDFS-14372 | NullPointerException | DataNode ID | × |
| YARN-4288 | NodeManager aborts | NodeManager ID | × |
| Unknown Bugs | | | |
| CASSANDRA-15758 | Thread crashes | Node status | ✓ |
| CASSANDRA-15548 | Data inaccessible | Node status | × |
| CASSANDRA-15546 | Data read failure | Node status | × |
| CASSANDRA-15437 | Decommission failure | Node status | × |
| CASSANDRA-11804[‡] | Data access failure | Node status | × |
| HDFS-15367 | File metadata inaccessible | NameNode status | ✓ |
| HDFS-15235 | NameNode crashes | NameNode status | ✓ |
| YARN-10301 | Fail to stop a YARN service | ResourceManager ID | ✓ |
| YARN-10294 | Misleading error message | Container's location | ✓ |
| YARN-10288 | Invalid state transition | Container's location | ✓ |
| YARN-10232 | Invalid state transition | Container's location | ✓ |
| YARN-10231 | Misleading error message | Container ID | ✓ |

[†]Column "Stop" shows whether the network partition needs to stop to trigger the bug. [‡]We did not know CASSANDRA-11804 before CoFI exposed it. This bug is previously reported by others in Cassandra-3.5. But the original bug reporter can no longer trigger it in later versions of Cassandra. We are the first one to report this bug in Cassandra-3.11.5.

As shown in Table 5.4, CoFI successfully detects all four known bugs using the workloads specified in the bug's JIRA report, demonstrating CoFI's effectiveness in detecting known partition bugs.

Table 5.4 also shows that, CoFI identifies 12 partition bugs using the interesting variables and the simple workloads (common user and admin operations) that we specified for each system (Table 5.2). All 12 bugs are previously unknown in the system versions we test. At the time of this writing, four of the unknown bugs (CASSANDRA-15548, CASSANDRA-11804, HDFS-15235, YARN-10288) have been confirmed by developers. The exposed unknown bugs have different symptoms, including severe failures like node crashes and data access failures. Note that these bugs only rely on a small set of interesting metadata, i.e., Cassandra's node status, HDFS's NameNode status, YARN's ResourceManager ID, container location, and container ID.

In Table 5.4, we can also see that CoFI is effective in exposing partition bugs that requires the network partition to stop at certain points. Specifically, 10 out of 16 bugs can only be triggered by stopping the network partition at certain timing. CoFI exposes these bugs by systematically stopping the network partition for each type of messages. On the contrary, it is challenging to expose these bugs using existing techniques that rely on developers to specify when the network partition starts and stops.

**False Positive Analysis**

Table 5.5 shows the detailed statistics of applying CoFI to the latest versions of the target systems. In total, CoFI reports 49 *unique* test failures in these systems (Column "Total"). 15 of these failures are caused by the unknown bugs listed in Table 5.4 (Column "Bug"). The remaining failures are mostly false positives (Column "False Positive"), while one failure cannot be reproduced for diagnosis (Column "Can't Reproduce").

111

| System | Bug | False Positive | Can't Reproduce♣ | Total |
|---|---|---|---|---|
| Cassandra-3 | 5 | 5 | 0 | 10 |
| HDFS-3 | $2^\dagger$ | 5 | 0 | 7 |
| HDFS-2 | $2^\dagger$ | 7 | 0 | 9 |
| YARN-3 | 5 | 12 | 0 | 17 |
| YARN-2 | $1^\ddagger$ | 4 | 1 | 6 |
| **Total** | **15** | **33** | **1** | **49** |

♣One of the test failures cannot be reproduced for diagnosis. †The two failures in HDFS-3 and the two failures in HDFS-2 share the same two root causes (HDFS-15367 and HDFS-15235). ‡The failure in YARN-2 shares the same root cause (YARN-10232) with one of the failures in YARN-3.

We further investigate the false positives reported by CoFI. We find that, most (28 out of 33) of these false positives are caused by our checkers asserting for operation success while the operation has to fail. For example, in one of the false positives in Cassandra, a data read with quorum consistency (2 out of 3) fails with a "NoHostAvailable" error. This failure matches with Cassandra's specification because the coordinator node for the read request is partitioned from the other two nodes. As a result, it does not have enough peers (hosts) to serve the request.

These false positives raise a challenge in generating oracles for fault injection tests. Specifically, the correct system behaviors may vary in different fault scenarios. For example, if the "NoHostAvailable" error occurs when only a non-coordinator node is partitioned, the failure is a bug because the coordinator should have enough peers to serve the read request. Automatically generating oracles for fault injection tests will be a challenge for the future research.

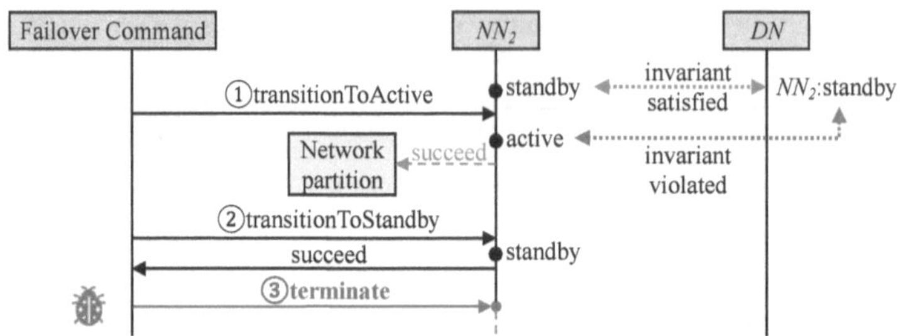


Figure 5.6: The Triggering Process of HDFS-15235.


**Case Study**

We now show an example of how partition bugs can occur under intricate network partition scenarios and how CoFI's choice of the partition starting points and the exploration of the stopping points help CoFI expose partition bugs.

Figure 5.6 shows a partition bug HDFS-15235, which is triggered by a temporary network partition that occurs when a failover attempt is being rolled back. This is a previously-unknown partition bug reported by CoFI. In a cluster with two NameNodes, $NN_2$ has just became active in a failover attempt (Step ①). Due to a network partition, $NN_2$ fails to respond to the failover command, which triggers a rollback (Step ②). Normally, as the network partition recovers, $NN_2$ should safely change back to standby. However, a bug in the rollback process unconditionally terminates $NN_2$ during the rollback (Step ③). As a result, the cluster loses a healthy NameNode only because of an untimely transient network partition!

CoFI triggers this bug when using the invariant that $NN_2$ and the DataNode in the cluster ($DN$) agree on $NN_2$'s status in consistent states. After $NN_2$ becomes active but before it informs *DN*, the system is inconsistent. At this point, CoFI starts a network partition on $NN_2$. During CoFI's systematic exploration of different partition stopping points, it will test stopping the network partition before Step ②, which then triggers the bug. In our experiment, CoFI exposes this bug using only 15 runs when testing HDFS-3. As this example shows, the correctness of a protocol implementation can be hard to analyze under intricate network partition scenarios. CoFI can help expose partition bugs in the implementation by systematically exploring different network partition scenarios. It is also worth noting that to trigger this bug the network partition needs to start and stop *in the middle of* one failover command issued by the admin. Therefore, injecting network partitions at the user operation level, i.e., starting and stopping the network partition before or after the failover command, cannot trigger this bug.

### 5.5.3   Comparing with Random Fault Injection

Table 5.6 compares the partition bugs triggered by CoFI and randomly injecting network partitions using the policy described in §5.5.1. Specifically, the table shows the bugs triggered by each approach (Column "CoFI" and Column "Random") as well as whether the bug requires stopping the network partition to trigger (Column "Stop"). As the table shows, CoFI is more effective in exposing partition bugs than random injection. Specifically, the random injection only triggerred 6 out of 12 bugs triggered by CoFI. Moreover, the random injection did not trigger any bug that is new to CoFI. It is also worth noting that if the random injection does not stop the network partition, 3 out of these 6 bugs will not be triggered.

To understand why random injection is not effective in triggering partition bugs, we further analyze the triggering process of four representative bugs (`CASSANDRA-15437`,

Table 5.6: Comparison between CoFI and the Random Fault Injection.

| Bug ID | Stop[†] | CoFI[‡] | Random[♣] |
|---|---|---|---|
| CASSANDRA-15758 | ✓ | ✓ | ✓ |
| CASSANDRA-15548 | × | ✓ | ✓ |
| CASSANDRA-15546 | × | ✓ | × |
| CASSANDRA-15437 | × | ✓ | ✓ |
| CASSANDRA-11804 | × | ✓ | ✓ |
| HDFS-15367 | ✓ | ✓ | ✓ |
| HDFS-15235 | ✓ | ✓ | × |
| YARN-10301 | ✓ | ✓ | × |
| YARN-10294 | ✓ | ✓ | × |
| YARN-10288 | ✓ | ✓ | × |
| YARN-10232 | ✓ | ✓ | × |
| YARN-10231 | ✓ | ✓ | ✓ |

[†]Column "Stop" shows whether the bug requires stopping the network partition to trigger. [‡]Column "CoFI" shows whether the bug is triggered by CoFI. [♣]Column "Random" shows whether the bug is triggered by the random fault injection.

Table 5.7: The Overhead of CoFI.

| System | Invariants | | Test Runs | |
| --- | --- | --- | --- | --- |
| | **Mined** | **Selected** | **Iterations** | **Time** |
| Cassandra-3 | 513 | 99 | 9,366 | 222h, 20m |
| HDFS-3 | 157 | 48 | 944 | 24h, 09m |
| HDFS-2 | 256 | 68 | 1,305 | 39h, 41m |
| YARN-3 | 51 | 14 | 1,151 | 240h, 11m |
| YARN-2 | 32 | 8 | 250 | 58h, 59m |
| **Total** | 1,009 | 237 | 13,016 | 585h, 20m |

HDFS-15367, HDFS-15235, and YARN-10232) to compute the probability to trigger them randomly. First, we assume that the node to partition is correctly selected. Then, based on a *concrete execution*, we compute the probability of selecting the right starting point of the network partition $P(start)$ and the conditional probability of selecting the right stopping point based on the selected starting point $P(end|start)$. Finally, the probability to randomly trigger a bug is computed as $P(bug) = P(start) \times P(end|start)$. We find that the two bugs triggered by both CoFI and the random injection have high likelyhoods to trigger ($P(CA\text{-}15437) = 12.65\%$, $P(HF\text{-}15367) = 8.87\%$), while the other two bugs only triggered by CoFI have much lower probabilities ($P(HF\text{-}15235) = 0.08\%$, $P(YN\text{-}10232) = 0.002\%$). Therefore, both our experiment and our analysis suggest that CoFI is more effective than random injection in triggering partition bugs.

## 5.5.4 Overhead Analysis

To measure the overhead of CoFI, we record several metrics while applying CoFI to detect unknown bugs. The metrics include the number of invariants mined and selected by CoFI, as well as the test iterations and wall clock time CoFI spends in testing each target system. Table 5.7 shows the values of these metrics.

In the fault injection stage, there are in total 13,016 test runs for all five system versions (Column "Iterations"), which takes about 585 hours to finish (Column "Time"). Specifically, the average time for each test run (Column "Time" / Column "Iterations") in Cassandra and HDFS is about 1 to 2 minutes. On average, YARN requires more than 10 minutes to finish one test run. This is because YARN employs a wait-and-retry mechanism for many operations. The test time can be shortened by configuring YARN to reduce the wait time and the number of max retries. Given that cloud systems are complicated, the above result demonstrates that CoFI is efficient to be used for in-house testing.

Table 5.7 also shows, in the invariant mining stage, CoFI mines 1,009 distributed program invariants from the target systems (Column "Mined"). After applying CoFI's invariant pruning strategy, only 237 invariants remain (Column "Selected"). That's said, about 76% of invariants are removed by CoFI's invariants pruning strategy, significantly reducing the number of invariants to test.

## 5.6  Summary

Partition bugs widely exist in cloud systems and cause cloud system failures. This chapter present consistency-guided fault injection (CoFI), a novel technique that injects network partitions to expose partition bugs in cloud systems. CoFI is the first fault injection technique that controls both the starting point and the stopping point of the injected network partition. Experiments with multiple popular cloud systems shows that CoFI is both effective in exposing partition bugs and efficient to be used in real world cloud system testing.

# Chapter 6: Conclusion and Future Work

This book makes contributions along three directions to address fault tolerance bugs, i.e., FTBugs, to improve the dependability of cloud systems. These three directions are understanding FTBugs, detecting FTBugs, and exposing FTBugs.

Along the direction of understanding FTBugs, this book presents one of the first comprehensive studies of a large set (210) of real world exception-related bugs, i.e., eBugs, collected from six widely deployed cloud systems. This study reveals multiple interesting findings regarding the triggering conditions, the root causes, and the impacts of eBugs in cloud systems. Most importantly, this study shows that the triggering condition of an exception provides vital information that can help prevent, expose and detect eBugs in cloud systems. The findings from this study have motivated and inspired the FTBug exposure and detection techniques presented in this book. Future reseach on preventing, exposing, and detecting FTBugs in cloud systems can also benefit from this study.

Along the direction of detecting FTBugs, this book proposes DIET and DECAF, two techniques to detect inaccurate exceptions. Both techniques detect inaccurate exceptions through identifying exception objects that have inconsistent feature values. Specifically, DIET employs a supervised approach to identify exception objects whose class and error message imply differnt types of faults. On the contrary, DECAF adopts an unsupervised approach to detect exception objects whose program context, exception class, and error message rarely co-appear. Experiments with multiple popular cloud systems show that both DIET and DECAF are effective in detecting inaccurate exceptions with different trade-offs.

Along the direction of exposing FTBugs, this book proposes CoFI, a new techqniue for injecting network partitions to expose partition bugs in cloud systems. Specifically, CoFI controls the timing of the network partition to thoroughly test a cloud system at inconsistent states. Experiments with multiple popular cloud systems show that CoFI is effective in exposing partition bugs. Specifically, CoFI exposes 12 previously unknown partition bugs in three popular cloud systems. Moreover, 8 of these 12 partition bugs require stopping the network partition to trigger.

This book has made contributions to address FTBugs in cloud systems. Of course, many open problems are left as future work.

One interesting problem is how to detect more types of FTBugs using the idea of inconsistency. Both DIET and DECAF detect inaccurate exceptions by identifying exception objects that have inconsistent features. What other inconsistencies do FTBugs have? How to exploit these inconsistencies to detect FTBugs? These are the interesting questions to be answered by future research.

Another interesting problem is how to expose more FTBugs in cloud systems. As discussed in Chapter 3, many fault types that can cause cloud system failures have not been covered by existing fault injection techniques. As a result, it is beneficial to design effective approaches to inject these faults to expose FTBugs in cloud systems. Connection refused, file not found, port conflict, and untimely interrupt can be the fault types to start with.

Although this book does not focus on preventing or fixing FTBugs, both are critical approaches to address FTBugs in cloud systems. Although preventing FTBugs is challenging, many techniques have been proposed recently. It is interesting to see how well these techniques are adopted by developers of real-world cloud systems. Existing techniques for fixing FTBugs only focus on a few types of FTBugs and the quality of the generated fixes can still be improved. Techniques for generating high quality fixes for more types of FTBugs can help developers quickly remove a bug after it is detected.

Addressing FTBugs in cloud systems is part of the answers to achieving dependable cloud systems. Configuration fault is another main cause of cloud system failures. How to design configuration parameters to reduce the posibility of configuration faults? How to detect incorrect re-configurations on the fly? How to tolerate re-configuration faults? These questions are interesting and must be answered in order to keep cloud systems dependable.